MIND VITAMINS

HOW TO MANAGE YOUR THOUGHTS FOR PEAK PERFORMANCE

Your personal 90 day plan

Erik Vermeulen

Mind Vitamins

Mind Vitamins: How to manage your thoughts for Peak Performance
Copyright© Erik Vermeulen and Ridgeline Consulting 2024

Ridgeline Consulting PTY LTD
198 Retief Ave, Centurion, 0157, South Africa
www.ridgelineza.com

ISBN: 978-0-7961-4569-7 **print**
        978-0-7961-4570-3 **ebook**

Editing, layout and typesetting by Erik Vermeulen
Cover by Erik Vermeulen and EP Digital South Africa

This book is the culmination of various thought-leadership pieces and articles written by Erik Vermeulen over a period of many years.

Thank you to all my clients, athletes, corporates and associates who have inspired me to think, write and be better.

To Sassenach
To Casey and Hayley
To everyone who inspires me

ABOUT THE AUTHOR

Meet Erik Vermeulen, a name synonymous with adventure and behavioural strategy. With a passion for exploring the unknown and understanding the complexities of human behaviour, Erik has carved a unique niche for himself in the world of adventure, leadership and performance. Born with an insatiable curiosity, he embarked on numerous thrilling expeditions across the diverse landscapes of South Africa and the world, seeking not only the thrill of the unknown but also a deeper understanding of human motivation & performance.

Erik's journey is not just about conquering mountains and traversing uncharted territories; it's about decoding the intricate patterns of human behaviour. As a seasoned behavioural strategist, he delves into the complexities of the human mind, unraveling the mysteries that govern our decisions and actions. His insights have not only enriched his own expeditions but have also been a guiding light for others, empowering them to navigate the intricate maze of life with confidence and purpose.

He stands as a beacon of inspiration, reminding us that the true essence of adventure lies not only in the external landscapes we explore but also in the uncharted territories of our own minds. His life's work is a testament to the harmonious blend of adventure and behavioural expertise, reminding us to embrace the unknown, both within and outside ourselves, and discover the extraordinary in the everyday.

In 2020, during the height of the COVID-19 pandemic, Erik co-created The Brightrock Battle of the Sports which saw him walk 800km over four expeditions with some of South Africa's sporting heroes to raise much needed funds in support vulnerable communities battling COVID.

FOREWORD

I first met Erik in a rather innocuous setting. My plane had arrived late for a talk at a speakers showcase and, surprisingly, Erik had volunteered to ride out to the airport and collect me. I say surprising because Erik was also on the program that day. These events are usually highly structured and precise and leave little time for a speaker to be 'dashing' off somewhere to pick up a potential 'competitor'. It was a welcome change and refreshing and I knew immediately that Erik was different.

I always believe you can tell far more about a person when he is doing something other than what he is paid to do. 'Off guard' as it were, it is in these moments that people's actions betray ultimately their thoughts and very frame of reference that governs their life. So it is apt, that in Erik's off moment, his behaviour would qualify him far more than any CV for what it is that he has written about. Erik is warm, friendly, interesting and articulate. But make no mistake; these qualities alone do not qualify someone to write on the importance of performance and the detailed intricacies of thought and the mind. Ultimately it is these very things that allow us to not only cope on a day to day basis, but also, to realise our awesome potential.

It is easy to lose sight of just how important managing our mind is, especially in the hub-bub mayhem of city life. Few people think uninterrupted on a daily basis, and if they do, it's for an hour at most. Instead, the agenda of the day dictates what and how we do things. Consequently most people are 'inefficient' thinkers without even realising it. We let our minds do things simply because that's how we have done it in the past.

003 Mind Vitamins

We think this way because that's how we thought about it before. But stop. Think for a moment about whether what you are doing is working. Is there a better way to do it, or a different way? Are you really using your mind as efficiently as you could?

My expedition to the South Pole brought home just how we take our minds for granted. Day after day, for more than two months, sometimes as long as 11 hours a day, I did nothing but think. And it was exhausting! Ahead of me loomed a journey that was interminable and more times than not, seemingly impossible. On many occasions I would recognise that my thinking was leading me down a dead end or a one track path to failure. So I would have to stop, reorder my thoughts, and break things down into smaller, manageable chunks. My mind developed little 'tricks' to deal with the enormity of it all. Sometimes I felt like I was 'cheating', but you see, that's what an efficient mind does…it cheats. But in a good way! It simply takes the enormous task of everyday life, and breaks it down into a process that is manageable. I guess it feels like cheating because so few people do it. It feels like you suddenly have the competitive edge. Without it I would have never made it to the South Pole, and similarly, without it, we will never get to a point in our lives where we are thriving!

Erik can help you do exactly that, thrive! His experience and research is widespread, detailed and varied. His insight is sharp and his manner easy going. More than anything, his style makes you really believe that this is something you can do, that its attainable, that's its intriguing, and ultimately, that's its necessary.

This book will take you on a journey that is every bit as illuminating as it is interesting. You will want to learn more, not just about yourself and your mind, but about Erik and those whose stories he shares. And, as Erik hints at, there is very little chance this will become another 'shelf-help' book! Indeed, it is more likely to end up firmly on your sled!

Alex Harris
Adventurer, Seven Summits Conqueror, Polar Explorer, Extreme Mountain Biker.

PREFACE

I never intended writing this book. Like a lot of great things in life it came my way when I least expected it. It came about through the utmost commitment not of myself to write it, but from a close friend and dedicated agent who hounded me relentlessly to write it.

I didn't have to sit for months to write it. I'd been putting these little pearls together over a period of time for an electronic newsletter published weekly by a sports magazine that I wrote a monthly Mind Performance column for.

In fact, the very thought of writing another book seemed daunting to me, particularly since book stores are flooded with "self-help" books that, once purchased normally become "shelf-help" books. The owners seldom read them, and once they have, the wisdom between the two covers tends to stay there – on the shelf – rather than making its way into the lives of the people who read the books.

So this is not intended to be another shelf-help book. My greatest wish is that you will find in this book a companion. A journeyman to accompany you on your trip (I use this word in every sense) to where you want to be. Don't set goals – dream. When children dream, they find ways to realise it. When adults set goals, they find obstacles to achieving them.

This book is focused on the dreams, not the obstacles, because what you focus on you will get.

The biggest compliment you can give me is not to recommend this book to everyone else, but to take some of these quotes, along with their story, and make them part of your daily vocabulary. Only in this way will they become real. Only in this way will you not be alone in success and alone in failure.

HOW TO USE THIS BOOK

It can be challenging to maintain a high level of focus on a single goal for an extended period, such as more than 90 days. Research in psychology and human behaviour suggests several reasons for this phenomenon.

First, the human brain tends to thrive on novelty and stimulation, and over time, the initial excitement or motivation associated with a goal can diminish.

Second, people often experience fatigue, both mentally and emotionally, when pursuing a single objective for an extended duration.

Lastly, setting goals within a 90-day timeframe aligns with our cognitive and emotional capacity, enabling individuals to maintain a higher level of commitment, motivation, and engagement.

This concept is one reason training programs often span 3 months – it accommodates the natural ebb and flow of motivation and aligns with the cognitive and emotional limitations of individuals, making it easier to sustain focus and motivation throughout the program.

Therefore this book is divided into 3 sections - each one containing daily motivational quotes and insights for one month. Each insight is followed by a blank journaling page allowing you to immediately capture your own state and the specific application of the nugget to your mindset at this specific moment.

If you use a pencil, you can recycle this book for every major event. These nuggets should be seen as the catalysts to your performance mindset.

CHAPTER 1

MIND MANAGEMENT PRINCIPLES

WHY MIND FOOD

Every action begins with a thought – not one thing you've done has been without thought. Therefore it stands to reason that, if you want to change your actions, you need to change your thinking. So let's quickly explore a little bit of physiology to clarify the body-mind dynamic.

Every movement you undertake is driven by the careful and systematic contraction and relaxation of muscles. Muscles work collaboratively to move limbs precisely through the intricate interaction of relaxation and contraction. This is the essence of movement.

Muscles though are driven by electrical impulses, called Action Potential, sent through the nervous system from our brain.

Thoughts, which drive our brain, originate from our thinking – a process that takes place in our mind as a result of our interaction with the world around us, which is facilitated through our 5 senses (see, hear, taste, touch and smell). As with everything in the universe, your mind is regulated by a set of firm principles, which I will briefly describe.

Here are 6 Mind Management Principles that, once you understand them, will allow you to apply the daily quotes in the rest of this book.

A Your Subconscious Mind Never Sleeps

Everything you have ever experienced has been stored in your sub-conscious. Even before you were born, your sub-conscious mind was active — absorbing the world around you and the environment of your mother.

To best understand this storage of experiences, it's best to liken your subconscious to a filing cabinet — a very big one. If you were to manage your filing cabinet, chances are you'd carefully assign a label to each file and then file them alphabetically, or numerically, or in some form of order which you'll understand. If you want information on your tax returns, for example, you'll look under "T" and get the file named "Tax Returns". Easy. And it won't take you more than a minute!

Now suppose I came to your highly organised filing system, empty all the contents on the floor and ask you to find your tax returns information, what will you do? You'd likely tell me to call next week while you sift through the pile of paper on the floor. And that's what your mind looks like. Unless you order the "files" and assign labels to experiences, the information becomes difficult to find.

If you want to improve your performance, lessen your mistakes and deliberately get the results you really want, you need to start creating order amongst your experiences and how they're stored in your sub-conscious.

YOUR MIND IS LIKE THE SOIL

What makes agriculture, and economies based on it, so successful is the relative predictability of what you're going to get. Assuming that climatic and soil conditions are stable; you always get what you planted. If you sow corn, that's what grows – every time! If you plant acorns, you get Oak trees – every time. The soil doesn't decide to give you pineapples if you've planted cashews. Neither does your mind.

Your mind will always give you back exactly what you put into it. So, as you work through this book, ask yourself what "seeds" you're planting in your mind as you go about your daily routine. If you work closely with others, look critically at the "seeds" you plant in their minds, because these words become self fulfilling prophesies. Take James for example. His co-workers always accused James of having poor time management skills and made effort tot remind him of his tardiness whenever they had a meeting scheduled or as a deadline approached. So James started hearing it from all angles, "James is always late."

To know how this becomes self-fulfilling, we need to have a look at how thoughts govern our actions. Take James, who has been told by several of his colleagues that he's always late. He gets a meeting reminder on his "Outlook" 10 minutes before the scheduled meeting – but his approach is what causes him to be late. His thought process is saying, "I've got ten minutes. But people expect me to be late so I'll see if I can finish this report I'm typing." 15 minutes later, he gets a call from the meeting room telling him that he's late – again.

011   Mind Vitamins

James was late not because he couldn't manage time. He's late because people expect him to be late and hence he lacks the focus to be on time. Suppose the opposite was true – and his colleagues often praised James for being on-time, well prepared and conscientious. His thrust mind pattern now becomes what people expect of him. When he gets the meeting reminder prior to his meeting, he gets up immediately as he now sub-consciously places high merit on being not only on time for the meeting, but actually a few minutes early.

Exercise

Take your thumb and forefinger and hold them about 5cm apart. Now place an elastic band over these two fingers and see how far apart you can pull them. You're probably doing this quite easily.

Keeping the elastic in place, relax your fingers and close your eyes. Repeat the following statement 10 times, saying the words slowly and adding emotion to the phrase. Once you have repeated the phrase, try and move your fingers apart against the elastic again. Repeat, "I am weak and worthless."

What has happened to your performance?

Next, close your eyes and recall from memory what you believe to be a pinnacle moment in your life. Your biggest success. Go there. Relive that event in your mind's eye, making sure you extract as much detail from that event as you can. "See" the faces of the people around you. Recall your friends and family who shared the moment with you. What were you wearing? How did the fabric feel on your skin? What was the weather like? What did the room feel like? How did it smell? How did you experience your facial expressions? Pick as much detail from the event that you can, and play it over in your mind like you're watching it on DVD as you like.

Now repeat the exercise with the elastic band.

What have you noticed about your performance?

YOUR MIND CAN ONLY HOLD ONE THOUGHT AT A TIME

Whenever I broach this subject in my seminars, females in the audience always challenge me. They are under the impression – along with most other people – that we can all multi-task.

Unfortunately, this is incongruent with how your mind works.

> *Exercise*
> *With a pen on a piece of paper, draw a number 6. Draw it nice and big. As you are now sitting, pick up the foot of the hand you write with. In other words, if you are right-handed, pick p your right foot. Make a clock-wise circle with this foot. After several seconds of making this circle, continue with the circle and then draw another "6" on the page. What has happened to your clock-wise foot circle?*

You will notice that your foot changed direction as you drew your 6. This is because your mind can only hold one thought at a time. While you were making the circle, that was the focus of your actions. But, when you started drawing the number 6, your dominant thought changed and that caused your foot to follow the new dominant thought - that being the counter-clockwise movement required to draw the number 6.

When we "multi-task" we effectively fragment our thought processes. We shuttle our thoughts and focus between the different activities we are engaged in, spending seconds at a time focusing on each of the tasks. As such, you've probably found yourself driving your vehicle while talking on your mobile phone.

Sooner or later, you may have found yourself somewhere along your route with little or no recollection of several kilometers of your journey. This happens when your focus was diverted from your surroundings by the intensity of your phone conversation.

Lack of focus and the fragmentation that occurs through our attempts to multi-task impact s negatively on our performance. When I first start working with athletes I ask them to complete a simple focus task. All I require from them is to spend one meal focusing only on the meal. No distractions. I need them to concentrate totally on their food. Its texture, taste, temperature, smells, and the feelings the food evokes etc. They find this incredibly difficult since most people have transformed meal times into social events, TV watching opportunities, discussion time with the family and time to meet other needs. This by the way is a major contributor to the increase in obesity!

Now think critically about the thoughts you put into your mind, or the thoughts that you are feeding the minds of others. What are you reading? What newspapers are you reading? How do you verbalise your intentions? Do you hold thoughts of possibility or thoughts of hurdles?

YOUR MIND WILL MOVE YOUR BODY IN THE DIRECTION OF YOUR DOMINANT THOUGHT

Your mind will find a way to move your body in the direction of your thinking, in the direction of your focus.

You saw this to a large extent in the previous exercise but I'd like you to think about it a little further. When you drive past the beach on a beautifully sunny summers day, I'm willing to bet you have let your eyes wonder from the road to some of the toned and tanned human specimens striding the pavement, or tanning on the beach. When you turned your attention to a passer-by, where did you vehicle go? Did it follow the road, or did it stray from the road in the direction of your focus?

If you like stretching yourself, taking risks and doing something "dangerous", why not enrol in a High Speed Driving Course. Here you will get to drive around a racetrack in an incredibly fast car, experience G-forces in the corners and get helmet-hair. More importantly though, you'll find out very quickly what happens to your car when you focus on the barriers on the outside of a corner!

Or go parachuting. On my first jump I was really worried about landing in the trees that surrounded the drop-zone. That was where I focused – and that was where I landed. In the trees.

Mind Vitamins

> *Exercise*
>
> *On a piece of paper, draw a big cross, with arms vertically and horizontal. Using a paper-clip and a piece of string, create a pendulum about the length of your forearm.*
>
> *Place both your elbows on a flat, sturdy surface, holding the string between the thumb and forefinger of your dominant hand.*
>
> *Steady your dominant hand with your other hand so that the pendulum is suspended directly above the centre of the cross. About 2 centimetres above the table.*
>
> *Now focus only on the paperclip. Do not move your hands. Looking intently at the paperclip, and with unwavering focus, I want you to move the paperclip from left to right (east to west). Keep repeating the instruction to yourself. Visualise the paperclip moving left to right, left to right… small movements at first, then getting bigger. Keep repeating the instruction and continue to visualise the result you want.*
>
> *Once you've got a real fluid movement going, change your instructions to decrease the extent of the swing. Ask the pendulum to stop. Slowly, gradually the "see" the movements get smaller and slower until, eventually, the pendulum stops swinging. Now "instruct" the paperclip to change direction. This time think of moving it North – South.*
>
> *Do not move your hands. Looking intently at the paperclip, and with unwavering focus, I want to move the paperclip from North to South, up and down. Keep repeating the instruction to yourself. Visualise the paperclip moving up and down, up and down… small movements at first, then getting bigger.*

Can you now reflect on what happened? Did the clip move? How far? How quickly? Could you hold your focus, or did you give up when you didn't get immediate results? Are you a bit overwhelmed? Or feel that this is "black magic"?

The truth is simple. You're not in a Star Wars movie, becoming a Jedi or using the force. What you observed, the movement you created was a simple result of physiology. The natural workings of your nervous system and normal originators of all actions are in play.

Muscles cause movement. Particularly the contraction and relaxation of muscles. When you need to bend your arm at the elbow, the first physiological process is the formation of a small electrical impulse in your brain, called an Action Potential. This charge is fired through your network of nerves, down your arm to your biceps and triceps muscles. The action potential will stimulate your biceps to contract, your triceps to relax and that results in the movement of your arm.

We can measure these impulses by placing electrodes on the muscles themselves, allowing neuroscientists to not only identify the presence of an Action Potential, but also to measure the strength of these electrical messengers. In patients with spinal injuries, the absence of these messengers will often be the first hint that doctors look for when making a diagnosis.

When you are holding your hands "motionless" and thinking about the movement of the pendulum, you are trying to actively inhibit the result of the Action Potentials that will cause your hands to move by trying to hold your hands still. So you diminish the strength of the messages. However, they are still there and would register on an electroencephalogram.

Your thoughts are producing the necessary Action Potential to result in slight movements that are commensurate with your thoughts. On an-almost microscopic level, there is movement in your hands. This is eventually translated into the movement you observe in the pendulum.

YOUR MIND CANNOT DISTINGUISH BETWEEN WHAT'S REAL AND WHAT'S IMAGINARY

Exercise

You'll need a friend or spouse to help you with this exercise.

Make sure you are sitting relaxed in a comfortable chair. Place your hands on the arms rests, sit back, close your eyes and relax. While you are in this position, ask your partner to read the following script out loud. Ask them to read it with feeling and emotion, in a calm, comforting voice. All you need to do is listen to the comforting voice of your companion.

"You have had a long and tiring day. It's been hot, rushed and uncomfortable. You arrive home, dump your bag at the front door, and head for the kitchen. You're really thirsty. You walk into the kitchen and over to the fridge. With your right hand, you reach out and open the fridge. You feel the cool air from inside the fridge on your face, and you feel the glare of the fridge light on your eyes. Looking into the fridge, you see three bright green, ripe lemons on the middle shelf. Take one of the lemons, close the fridge door and walk over to the counter. Put the lemon down on the counter. Now slowly open the cutlery drawer, hearing the metal rattle and the rollers stick as you open it. Reach in and take out the sharpest knife you have. Holding the lemon on the counter, slice through it and see the two halves falling away from each other. Pick up one half of the lemon, bring it up to your lips and squeeze ice-cold lemon juice into your mouth."

What happened to you physically at the end of this exercise? If you were even remotely focused on the words, thoughts and ideas of the voice speaking to you, your body would have reacted in the same it does when you are REALLY putting lemon juice in your mouth.

Your body responded as it does when you are exposed to REAL lemon juice. Yet there isn't a lemon near you. Why is this? Why is it that sportsmen, employees, team members and "normal" people can be manipulated by the thoughts and ideas of others? Especially when these are vocalised and directed at people.

The reason is that your mind cannot distinguish between what is real, and what it imagines. The imagination is so powerful that it can – and does – affect physiology. This can of course only happen if you have previous experience of the emotion / event / feeling that you are trying to elicit.

I can have you imagine all day that you are at -20 degrees Celcius while traversing the Antarctic, but if you do not know what -20 degrees feels like, you can't replicate the physiology. It's all relative though. We may have eaten sour lemons, or hot chillies, and that would be enough to elicit the response. Remember that all your experiences are filed in your sub-conscious. They're there, ready to be drawn upon. But only if you know where you "filed" them.

When working on visualisation techniques as part of a pre-match routine, I ran an informal experiment. The usual pre-match routine involved the players relaxing and listening to a relaxation CD and I would call out certain set-pieces or game scenarios while the players were in a relaxed. The players involved in each phase would respond by twitching their legs, arms and eyes. Others would remain almost motionless and relaxed. Even though these were only imaginary scenarios, the players behaved as they would have on the field - in micro-movements.

The same happens when we dream whilst asleep.

YOUR MIND CANNOT OPERATE IN NEGATIVES

Whatever you do, do not think of pink elephants!

What are you thinking about right now?

90% of the population will say Pink Elephants. Even after you were clearly asked not to! Yet this is symptomatic of much of the communication we are subject to. Both as a receiver and as a sender of verbal messages. How do our clear messages not to do something translate so effectively into the action we wish people to avoid? The answer is simple.

We are human beings and as such we are designed to do things. People (even when they appear outwardly lazy and disinterested) are intrinsically programmed to do. As such, the verbal cues we follow, need to be structured to bear this in mind. When we listen to, read or interpret instructions the first thing we become interested in is what we are required to do. Therefore we will always look for the Verb first. In the case of the example above, "THINK".

As soon as we know what the verb is, we then need to look for the subject. What am I required to think of? In this case we find the subject pretty quickly, and quite amusing so it immediately moves us to action due to the curiosity factor is elicits.

2

CHAPTER 2

THE FIRST 30 DAYS

2

#1

WHEN I FEEL MYSELF TIRING, I CLOSE MY EYES AND REALISE MY FRIENDS ARE MY ENERGY

In the 1930's an American businessman, Napoleon Hill, was mentored by the great Andrew Carnegie. Several of the great business minds of the time got together on a regular basis and they soon discovered that they started to draw on each other's energy, ideas and success. This group came to be known as a "mastermind group"

You should be setting up your own "mastermind group" with your coach and training partners. Why do you think that adventure-racing teams accomplish so much more than individuals? They draw on each other's encouragement and energy.

Get together regularly with about 5 -7 training buddies (or colleagues) – some stronger and some weaker than you – to not only train together & brainstorm, but also to socialize. Of course if you want unwavering support from your wife / girlfriend / significant other, involve them in your mastermind group from time-to-time.

#1 WHEN I FEEL MYSELF TIRING, I CLOSE MY EYES AND REALISE MY FRIENDS ARE MY ENERGY

Reflect on the Role of Friends in Your Life: Take a moment to close your eyes, just as the quote suggests, and reflect on the importance of your friends in your life. How have your friends been a source of energy and support for you during challenging times? What specific experiences or moments come to mind when you think about your friends being a source of energy for you? Write about these experiences and the emotions they evoke.

Building Stronger Connections: Reflect on the quality of your friendships and the role they play in your life. Are there specific friends who consistently energize you more than others? What characteristics or qualities do these friends possess that make them such a positive influence on your energy levels? How can you nurture and strengthen these friendships, and what steps can you take to deepen your connections with those who uplift you when you're feeling tired?

#2

SUCCESS IS DUE LESS TO ABILITY THAN PASSION. THE WINNER IS THE ONE WHO GIVES HIS ENDEAVOUR BODY AND SOUL

Every so-often I hear athletes lament that they are not "natural athletes". But what is a "natural athlete"? Contrary to belief, we all have pretty much the same abilities.

Genetic differences account for only about 5 – 10% of performance. By far the biggest influence is commitment, dedication, training and discipline. This is what top athletes have more of. If you want to perform – at whatever level, you need to ask yourself if you're willing to give your endeavour body and soul. True commitment to a result only occurs when you cross the line and you cannot deliver another pedal turn, another paddle stroke, or put one more foot in front of the other.

Passion, when translated from its Latin origin, means "to suffer". To best understand commitment, consider your breakfast of bacon and eggs. The chicken is involved, but the pig is totally and absolutely committed. Be a pig for your performance.

#2 SUCCESS IS DUE LESS TO ABILITY THAN PASSION. THE WINNER IS THE ONE WHO GIVES HIS SPORT BODY AND SOUL

Explore your own definition of passion and how it relates to your work.
Consider what activities or aspects of your job ignite your passion.
Reflect on moments in your career when you felt most passionate about your work.
How does your level of commitment and dedication affect your performance and success in your field?

Explore the potential for aligning your passion with your career objectives.
Consider whether there are any adjustments or changes you could make in your work to better leverage your passion.
Identify specific actions you can take to invest more of yourself into your professional endeavours.

#3

A VICTORY IS DEFINED NOT BY WHAT HAPPENS BETWEEN THE START AND THE FINISH LINE, BUT BY WHAT HAPPENS BEFORE THE START LINE

What you do in preparation for performance is far more important than what you do during a race or event. It is your attitude toward performance away from the limelight, hidden from the public eye that defines your race.

Lance Armstrong laid the foundation for his Tour de France victories in the winter and spring, training in the snow, wind and rain. Average sportsmen and women are more concerned about how they look during the event, what they wear and who they hang out with than with the necessary "behind-the-scenes" preparation. Preparation away from the public eye is what lays the foundation for top performances.

Stephen Covey had a point when he wrote that "Private victories always precede Public victories".

#3 A VICTORY IS DEFINED NOT BY WHAT HAPPENS BETWEEN THE START AND THE FINISH LINE, BUT BY WHAT HAPPENS BEFORE THE START LINE

Consider opportunities for enhancing your pre-start line preparations.

Are there specific habits, routines, or strategies you can implement to better position yourself for success in your endeavours? Think about adjustments you can make to your approach and mindset.

#4

SOMETHING IN HUMAN NATURE CAUSES US TO START SLACKING OFF AT OUR MOMENT OF GREATEST ACCOMPLISHMENT. AS YOU BECOME SUCCESSFUL YOU WILL NEED A GREAT DEAL OF SELF-DISCIPLINE NOT TO LOSE YOUR SENSE OF BALANCE, HUMILITY AND COMMITMENT

Why is it that so many people stop to celebrate success when there's still so much to achieve? One of my athletes achieved 9% body fat and the best shape of his life in December in preparation for Ironman. Only to slack off totally and not even make it to the start!

Yes, we should celebrate small successes, BUT we should also never stop improving. We sell ourselves short so often – believing that we are at our peak and that things cannot get better. The cornerstone for Constant and Never-ending Improvement believes that if you're in great shape now, how can you get into better shape?

Success is the truest test of commitment and balance.

#4

SOMETHING IN HUMAN NATURE CAUSES US TO START SLACKING OFF AT OUR MOMENT OF GREATEST ACCOMPLISHMENT. AS YOU BECOME SUCCESSFUL YOU WILL NEED A GREAT DEAL OF SELF-DISCIPLINE NOT TO LOSE YOUR SENSE OF BALANCE, HUMILITY AND COMMITMENT

What are some past instances in your life when you noticed yourself slacking off or becoming complacent after achieving a significant accomplishment?

_____
_____
_____
_____
_____
_____
_____
_____
_____
_____
_____
_____
_____
_____
_____
_____
_____

#5

WHEN YOU LOSE, MAKE SURE YOU DON'T LOSE THE LESSON

I see it with the teams I work with. Whenever they win (which for some of them is sometimes about or above 75% of the time) they talk about the victory for hours (even days) after the event. But when they lose, or they don't get the outcome they desire, it gets swept under the carpet as soon as possible.

Make sure that when you don't get the outcome you desire, you spend some time determining why. By conducting an "after-action" review – particularly after a bad result – you begin true learning. When you learn from your mistakes, you reduce the number you can make in the future, thereby increasing your chances of producing better performances.

#5 WHEN YOU LOSE, MAKE SURE YOU DON'T LOSE THE LESSON

Reflect on a Recent Loss: Think of a recent experience where you faced a setback or loss, whether it's in your personal life, career, or a specific goal. Describe the situation and your initial emotional response to it. How did you feel when you first encountered the loss?

Identifying the Lesson: Explore what lessons you can draw from the loss you experienced. Consider what insights, knowledge, or personal growth emerged as a result. How did this setback provide you with an opportunity to learn or grow? Be specific about the lessons you've gained.

Application of the Lesson: Reflect on how you can apply the lessons learned from your past losses to your future endeavours. What practical steps can you take to ensure that you don't lose the valuable insights gained when facing setbacks? How can you turn these lessons into a source of strength and resilience in your life moving forward?

#6

SUCCESS IN ALMOST ANY FIELD DEPENDS MORE ON ENERGY AND DRIVE THAN IT DOES ON INTELLIGENCE

Remember when you were new in your chosen sport? Or when you attempted something new for the first time? Most people seek out "experts", or go online to find out as much as they possibly can. They read up on techniques, spend hours analysing their paddle stroke etc. Sure, all the info helps, but never allow it to become the focus of your training.

Besides, "smart" people look for reasons why things are not possible. People with energy, go out and do it anyway, only to find out that what they have just achieved "was not possible". Want proof… Roger Bannister and the 4-minute mile. Put more energy and drive into your sport – fitness and training will outweigh technique at most levels of competition. Time spent analysing will always be better spent DOING.

Now go out there and "just do it"

#6 SUCCESS IN ALMOST ANY FIELD DEPENDS MORE ON ENERGY AND DRIVE THAN IT DOES ON INTELLIGENCE

Strategies for Boosting Energy and Drive

Think about ways you can enhance your energy and drive in pursuit of your goals. What strategies or habits can you develop to maintain a high level of motivation and determination? How can you leverage your existing intelligence while also nurturing your energy and drive to achieve even greater success in your chosen field?

_____
_____
_____
_____
_____
_____
_____
_____
_____
_____
_____
_____
_____
_____
_____
_____
_____

#7

WE MUST NOT ALLOW OTHER PEOPLE'S LIMITED PERCEPTIONS TO DEFINE US

I can guarantee you that since you were able to walk other people have defined who you've become. How many times in your life have you heard the word "Don't"? Don't do this… Don't do that… Don't go there.

Or, maybe someone has said to you "You can't do this… You'll never be that… You're too fat / thin / short."? When we hear something often enough it becomes imprinted in our sub-conscious, AND WE BEGIN TO BELIEVE IT. When it comes to our endeavours too, people close to us develop expectations and often inadvertently transfer those onto us. They sell us short.

Make sure that you define yourself through your true abilities, energy and determination. Create your own powerful expectations of yourself and what you can achieve. Get a coach who believes in you if you have to, but make sure you define who you are.

#7 WE MUST NOT ALLOW OTHER PEOPLE'S LIMITED PERCEPTIONS TO DEFINE US

Defining Self-Worth
Consider your own sense of self-worth and self-identity. How do you perceive yourself independently of external judgments? What qualities, values, or achievements make you who you are? How can you strengthen your self-definition so that it remains resilient against external opinions?

Empowering Self-Definition
Think about actions and practices that can help you stay true to your own self-definition. What steps can you take to reinforce your self-confidence and self-awareness? How can you maintain a sense of authenticity and self-determination, regardless of what others may think or say about you?

#8

SOME PEOPLE MAKE THINGS HAPPEN, SOME WATCH WHILE THINGS HAPPEN, AND OTHERS WONDER WHAT HAPPENED

In sport, business and life, at any level, you need to take control of yourself and as many of the variables that affect your performance as you possibly can. If you are not proactive in doing this you become one of those people who watch as things happen around them.

If you lose even more control, end up wondering what happened as your performance suffers, and at the worst, you fail to complete events, achieve the levels of performance you hoped for and you quit.

#8 SOME PEOPLE MAKE THINGS HAPPEN, SOME WATCH WHILE THINGS HAPPEN, AND OTHERS WONDER WHAT HAPPENED

Assessing Your Proactivity
Reflect on your recent professional endeavours and activities. In which category do you find yourself - someone who makes things happen, someone who watches while things happen, or someone who wonders what happened? Provide specific examples to illustrate your role in various situations. What motivates or hinders your ability to take initiative and make things happen in your work?

Developing a Proactive Mindset
Consider your professional goals and aspirations. How can you shift your mindset and behaviour towards becoming more of a "maker" rather than an observer or a wonderer? What strategies or habits can you develop to cultivate a proactive approach in your leadership or work? Identify concrete steps you can take to be more intentional and action-oriented in achieving your objectives.

#9

ACTION SHOULD CULMINATE IN WISDOM

The second worst thing that can happen to an athlete is to have bad race. There will be days when nothing seems to gel, when your legs are heavy, when you just don't feel like it. A few years ago I had one of "those" days after my wife got me doing some DIY in the garden involving paving stones the day before a race. That was the longest 110km EVER on a bike.

The worst thing that can happen though is not learning from your actions. So many people go from one experience to another without actively making an effort to learn from it. Ensure that every event, projects or team you participate in is followed by an "after-action review". This way you can eliminate repetitive mistakes and, more importantly, keep doing what works.

Good actions, breed good habits, which breed consistent good results.

#9 ACTION SHOULD CULMINATE IN WISDOM

The Role of Learning and Growth

Explore how the concept of continuous learning and growth relates to the idea that action should culminate in wisdom. What are some intentional practices or habits you can adopt to facilitate personal and professional growth through your actions? How can you ensure that your actions contribute to your overall wisdom and understanding?

#10

PAIN IS TEMPORARY. QUITTING LASTS FOREVER

It is as inevitable as tomorrow's sunrise that there will be a moment in any event and in training, that you suffer – both mentally and physically. Lance Armstrong's words have become a strong anchor for me when this happens.

When Lance Armstrong coined this phrase, he explained that quitting when things get tough would be taking the easy way out. Once you've quit (as he could have during chemotherapy) you can never un-quit. You can never go back to that exact moment in the race, that exact moment in time to find out what would have happened if you didn't quit.

The pain however is temporary. At the top of this hill, around the next corner, when you reach the finish line, the pain will stop. It will end. It will soon be dulled by the feeling of victory, anaesthetized by the sense of accomplishment.

#10 PAIN IS TEMPORARY. QUITTING LASTS FOREVER

Reflecting on Past Challenges
Think about a time in your life when you faced a challenging situation or obstacle in your pursuit of a goal. Describe the pain or discomfort you experienced during that period. How did you overcome it, and what did you learn from the experience? How can you apply this lesson to your current goals or any future challenges you may encounter?

Creating a Resilience Plan
Considering the idea that pain is temporary and quitting has lasting consequences, what strategies can you put in place to increase your resilience and determination when facing difficulties in your personal or professional life? How can you remind yourself of the long-term consequences of quitting in moments when you're tempted to give up? Describe practical steps you can take to maintain your commitment and motivation.

#11

USE WHAT TALENTS YOU POSSESS; THE WOODS WOULD BE VERY SILENT IF NO BIRDS SANG EXCEPT THOSE THAT SING BEST

The beauty about multi-sport – in fact just about any endurance event – is to be found at the start and finish line. Have a look at the diversity of body shapes around. The number of less-than-perfect physiques present always amaze me – even at the end of Comrades or Ironman. The statistics show that less than 2% of athletes at the start of an event have the ability to win it. So why is everyone else there?

Because, for most of us, we want to use the talents we have. We want to edge from our comfort zone and see what we are capable of. Do one thing every day that scares you. Explore. Use your talents of mobility and your senses to liven the world around you. You make endurance events possible – not the elite athletes!

Run your race, enter your event, because without you there will not be an event!

#11 USE WHAT TALENTS YOU POSSESS; THE WOODS WOULD BE VERY SILENT IF NO BIRDS SANG EXCEPT THOSE THAT SING BEST

What unique talents or strengths do you possess that you may have been underutilizing or hesitant to showcase?

_____

How can you apply this quote to your current goals or challenges?

#12

DON'T COUNT THE DAYS; MAKE THE DAYS COUNT

We've already marked our favorite events on the calendar. For the real tough ones, we've worked out our periodisation schedule and then…

Why do some people then sit back and count the days? I know athletes who can tell me to the day how much time there is before their next big event, but then also tell my why they didn't train today. Why count the days in such an obsessive way? I say obsessive because that's what it becomes. Folks focus on time, instead of what they're going to do with that time. Remember that each BEHAG (Big Hairy Achievable Goal) will consist of many smaller goals.

Condition yourself to do something everyday that will move you in the direction of your goal. It doesn't have to be 80km on the bike, or an hour on the water in near freezing temperatures. Do anything that is related to achieving what you want. Do it today, because tomorrow may not be here.

Mind Vitamins

#12   DON'T COUNT THE DAYS; MAKE THE DAYS COUNT

How can a mindset of making each day count contribute to your overall performance and mental resilience?

_____
_____
_____
_____
_____
_____
_____
_____

What potential distractions or obstacles can derail your focus on making each day count, and how can you mitigate them?

_____
_____
_____
_____
_____
_____
_____
_____

#13

SOMETIMES BEING PUSHED TO THE WALL GIVES YOU THE MOMENTUM NECESSARY TO GET OVER IT

We've all read or heard those miraculous stories about the little old lady who rushes out the front door to lift up a 1500kg car that's parked on her two year-old granddaughter. Yes, the "fight-or-flight" response.

When we panic, our body responsively releases adrenalin to allow us to react to the "danger" we're faced with. As athletes, we have the ability to release adrenalin at will – for example in the final 100m of a MTB sprint to the finish. In the same way that we can manipulate our mind to combat fatigue through auto-suggestion, so we can use our physiology to our advantage in a sprint.

Here's what you do. The moment you want to release the shot of adrenalin, tighten your sphincter muscles suddenly – as you would involuntarily when you get a big fright. Your body will respond by assuming you are in danger and would therefore release adrenalin.

#13 SOMETIMES BEING PUSHED TO THE WALL GIVES YOU THE MOMENTUM NECESSARY TO GET OVER IT

What Was a Time When You Felt Pushed to the Wall? Reflect on a specific instance in your life when you experienced significant pressure or adversity. Describe the situation, the emotions you felt, and the challenges you encountered.

How Did You Respond to This Pressure? Explore how you reacted to the situation described in the first question. Did you feel motivated to take action? Did you find a surge of energy or determination? Or did you feel overwhelmed and stressed? What were the key factors that influenced your response?

What Did You Learn from This Experience? Reflect on the outcomes and lessons from the situation in question. Did you overcome the challenge? If so, how did you do it? What skills, strengths, or support systems did you tap into? If you didn't overcome it, what could you have done differently? What broader lessons can you draw from this experience about finding motivation in difficult circumstances?

_____

_____

_____

_____

_____

_____

_____

_____

_____

_____

_____

_____

_____

_____

_____

_____

_____

_____

_____

#14

ONE WHO WRESTLES WITH US STRENGTHENS OUR NERVES, AND SHARPENS OUR SKILL. OUR ANTAGONIST IS OUR HELPER.

In the 1960's physiologists, sports scientists and athletes agreed that it is impossible to break 4 minutes in running the mile. They told stories of how human lung function is inadequate, that man's oxygen delivery system will collapse, that imminent death will result if someone were to run 1600m in under 4 minutes.

Then, one day, Roger Bannister came along and did it. There are countless other examples I history of "proof" that something was not possible – only for it to be done! Our antagonists, our detractors, the people who tell us that we're too fat, too old, too busy, too unfit, not experienced enough are the ones who drive our performance.

Embrace your competitors. They provide a powerful external influence over our mindset, our preparation, and ultimately our performance.

#14 ONE WHO WRESTLES WITH US STRENGTHENS OUR NERVES, AND SHARPENS OUR SKILL. OUR ANTAGONIST IS OUR HELPER.

Who or What Has Been Your Antagonist or Challenge?
Reflect on a person, situation, or challenge that you've considered as an antagonist in your life. Describe this antagonist and how it has made you feel. What specific struggles or obstacles did you face?

How Has Facing this Antagonist Benefited You?
Explore the ways in which dealing with this antagonist has had a positive impact on your personal growth and development. Have you learned new skills, gained resilience, or developed greater determination as a result of this challenge? How has it made you stronger or more skilled?

#15

IF YOU DON'T HAVE CONFIDENCE, YOU'LL ALWAYS FIND A WAY NOT TO WIN

An athlete related his Ironman experience to me recently. "Guys that are way beneath me finished ahead of me!" he lamented. He then continued with several excuses as to why he'd had a bad race. I call this disease excusitis. Guess what, if they really were beneath his ability and preparation they would not have finished ahead of him!

People who don't have self-confidence will never get confidence anywhere else. Not in races, not in performance enhancing drugs, not in weaker training partners. People without confidence will always find ways not perform well. People without confidence will always find something, or someone to blame.

Performance on the field begins with confidence off it.

#15 IF YOU DON'T HAVE CONFIDENCE, YOU'LL ALWAYS FIND A WAY NOT TO WIN

Reflect on Past Successes: Think about a time when you felt extremely confident and performed exceptionally well. Describe the situation and what contributed to your confidence. What did you do differently during that successful performance?

_____

_____

_____

_____

_____

_____

_____

_____

Identify Confidence Blockers: Now consider factors that have the potential to erode your confidence. It could be self-doubt, fear of failure, external pressure, or any other factor. Identify these blockers and consider ways to address or overcome them.

_____

_____

_____

_____

_____

_____

_____

#16

IMPROVE YOUR SELF-DISCIPLINE BY REMINDING YOURSELF OF THE RESULTS YOU WILL ACHIEVE THROUGH IT

Here it is, that big word – Self Discipline. Don't panic! In my book, self-discipline equals nothing more than Habits. So, get into the habit (pardon the pun) of forming strong habits.

Psychologists tell us that it takes 21 days to form a habit. If you repeat an action for 21 days, that action becomes ingrained in your neural pathways.

One of my clients, not an athlete but a Manager at a big pharmaceutical company, wanted to lose weight. He related his solution to maintaining his self-discipline during his weight-loss programme, particularly the exercise and training aspects. Whenever he lacked the motivation to go to gym, he reminded himself how good he would feel AFTER his workout. This link with an emotion, coupled with his routine of training at the same time everyday allowed for uncharacteristic self-discipline.

Within three weeks, your habits are established. You really only need "self-discipline" for three weeks, thereafter you'll be cruising on autopilot. By the way, this guy lost 38kg, and kept it off!

#16 IMPROVE YOUR SELF-DISCIPLINE BY REMINDING YOURSELF OF THE RESULTS YOU WILL ACHIEVE THROUGH IT

Accountability Partners: Who in your trusted circle can you team up with as accountability partners? Regular check-ins and discussions about progress can be motivating and reinforcing.

Celebrate Self-Discipline Milestones: Recognise and celebrate self-discipline milestones and achievements. What could these milestones be?

#17

THERE ARE MANY SUCCESSFUL TALKERS IN LIFE. THERE ARE FAR FEWER SUCCESSFUL DOERS

We all know these people. They're the ones who join in training sessions and never shut up. They're the ones always telling you what they did, how they did it, how hard they did it, etc. You find them at the office too!

I believe there are two types of people – those who talk about things and those who do things. Don't be one of the talkers – be a do-er. You can't do things while you're talking. Besides, people don't catch what you say, they catch what you do.

Actions speak much louder than words so don't give away your power by telling everyone what you're doing.

#17 THERE ARE MANY SUCCESSFUL TALKERS IN LIFE. THERE ARE FAR FEWER SUCCESSFUL DOERS

What specific actions or projects have I talked about or planned but not yet acted upon?
List 3 of these projects or actions and explore the reasons behind the lack of follow-through. Are there common themes or obstacles that have prevented you from taking action?

What steps can I take today to move from talking to doing in one of these areas?
Break down the goal into smaller, manageable tasks, and set a timeline for each step. This encourages a commitment to action and provides a practical roadmap for achieving it.

_____
_____
_____
_____
_____
_____
_____
_____
_____
_____
_____
_____
_____
_____
_____
_____
_____
_____

#18

CHALLENGES MAKE YOU DISCOVER THINGS ABOUT YOURSELF YOU NEVER KNEW. THEY MAKE YOU GO BEYOND THE NORM

A ship anchored in the harbour is safe. It also never goes anywhere. When you stay with what you know, you also never learn anything new. When you don't learn new things you stagnate, and as any canoeist will tell you, water that stagnates smells and evaporates. People are the same.

Try something new every few months. A new sport, a new supplement, a new training programme. Stimulate your mind, your body and your muscles. Challenge your perceptions. Try some cross-training. Not only will you discover new things about yourself, you'll also discover new things about your sport and the limits you can push beyond.

#18 CHALLENGES MAKE YOU DISCOVER THINGS ABOUT YOURSELF YOU NEVER KNEW. THEY MAKE YOU GO BEYOND THE NORM

Recall a recent challenge or obstacle you faced in your life. What specific aspects of yourself did you discover during this experience?

_____
_____
_____
_____

How did you go beyond your usual limits or comfort zone when facing this challenge?

_____
_____
_____
_____

What did you learn from this challenge that you can apply to future obstacles or goals?

_____
_____
_____
_____

In what ways can you intentionally seek out challenges or opportunities for personal growth in your life?

_____
_____
_____
_____

#19

ONCE YOU CAN SEE, TOUCH AND FEEL YOUR OBJECTIVE, ALL YOU HAVE TO DO IS PULL BACK AND PUT ALL YOUR STRENGTH BEHIND IT, AND YOU'LL HIT YOUR TARGET EVERY TIME

I am always amazed at the small number of people who have definite, documented objectives. Some go through the effort to enter events – that's their goal. But almost none train deliberately.

Don't just set event goals. See your objective before each training session, live it and don't settle for anything less.

This attitude saw Lance (Armstrong) ride an Alpine climb twice in training – simply because he wasn't happy with the way he rode it the first time.

Put all your focus and strength into your training session goal. Once you've learnt to do this effectively, the event will take care of itself.

#19

ONCE YOU CAN SEE, TOUCH AND FEEL YOUR OBJECTIVE, ALL YOU HAVE TO DO IS PULL BACK AND PUT ALL YOUR STRENGTH BEHIND IT, AND YOU'LL HIT YOUR TARGET EVERY TIME

What is your current objective or goal, and how clearly can you envision it, both in detail and emotionally?
How well can you visualise and emotionally connect with this goal? A clear and vivid mental image can be a powerful motivator.

How are you currently aligning your efforts and resources to hit your target?
Are you fully committing their strength and resources toward achieving the objective? Are there areas where you might be holding back or not giving your best effort?

What adjustments or improvements can you make to increase your chances of hitting the target consistently?
Are there specific skills, resources, or strategies that need enhancement or modification? What can you do to increase the likelihood of consistently hitting your targets?

#20

THERE IS A REAL MAGIC IN ENTHUSIASM. IT SPELLS THE DIFFERENCE BETWEEN MEDIOCRITY AND ACCOMPLISHMENT

It's very easy to be enthusiastic about something when it's new and when it is aspirational. How many of us dream about being able to pursue our sport, hobby or passion on a full-time basis?

Let's be honest, the easiest way to get excited abut your sport is to get some new equipment – a new bike, new shoes – know what I mean? The magic of enthusiasm though lies not in the feeling itself, but rather in the sustainability of your enthusiasm. You need to find something in your endeavours that fires your enthusiasm and gets you excited about your performance.

Look within, look at your challenges, look at your training buddies and find infinite enthusiasm. When I find it, I'll be bottling it at its source and selling it!

#20 THERE IS A REAL MAGIC IN ENTHUSIASM. IT SPELLS THE DIFFERENCE BETWEEN MEDIOCRITY AND ACCOMPLISHMENT

In what ways can you ignite or reignite enthusiasm in yourself and your team?
How can you create an environment that fosters excitement and energy around shared goals? What can you do to inspire and motivate others?

_____
_____
_____
_____
_____
_____
_____
_____

Can you identify specific moments in your career when enthusiasm played a crucial role in your accomplishments?
What specific actions or decisions were influenced by your enthusiasm, and how did this impact the outcome?

_____
_____
_____
_____
_____
_____
_____
_____

#21

A SMILE RELEASES ALL THE MAJOR FACIAL MUSCLES AND SETS OFF AN EMOTIONAL CHAIN REACTION THAT HELPS YOU FEEL GOOD

Your mind cannot distinguish between reality and what you imagine to be real. I often ask my corporate clients if they would prefer people to be sincerely miserable or insincerely happy.

As an athlete, if you're unhappy with yourself, with your training and with your performance, you can only improve it by changing your emotional state first. As you make this change, your physical state will also change for the better. You'll become more energised, feel more resourceful and become more motivated.

The best place to start is to smile and to remind yourself of everything you do have rather than to focus on what you don't have.

#21 A SMILE RELEASES ALL THE MAJOR FACIAL MUSCLES AND SETS OFF AN EMOTIONAL CHAIN REACTION THAT HELPS YOU FEEL GOOD

Reflect on a recent experience when you genuinely felt happy and content. How did your body and mind respond to this happiness, and how did it impact your stress levels?
Did you notice a relaxation of facial muscles, as the statement suggests? How did this happiness influence your stress levels and overall motivation?

_____
_____
_____
_____
_____
_____
_____
_____

Think about a challenging task or goal you're currently working on. How can you incorporate moments of happiness into your daily routine to make the process more enjoyable and less stressful?
How can these moments of happiness alleviate stress and create a more motivating and productive atmosphere?

_____
_____
_____
_____
_____
_____
_____
_____

#22

CHERISH YOUR VISIONS AND DREAMS, AS THEY ARE THE CHILDREN OF YOUR SOUL, THE BLUE-PRINTS OF YOUR ULTIMATE ACHIEVEMENTS

Coaches are always on about goal-setting. Yet less than 5% of the population have written goals. No wonder goal-setting becomes difficult. Think back to when you were 5 years old – or look at your own kids. When they "set goals" they call them "dreams". (Go ahead, ask jnr what he wants for his birthday!)

You also had those dreams when you started your sport, your career, when you started the season, and when you go to bed at night. Problem is, there are plenty of people around who give us all the reasons why we can't achieve our dreams. So we begin to believe what we hear all the time.

Go find your 5 year-old. Dream. Often. Big. Share your dreams.

#22 CHERISH YOUR VISIONS AND DREAMS, AS THEY ARE THE CHILDREN OF YOUR SOUL, THE BLUEPRINTS OF YOUR ULTIMATE ACHIEVEMENTS

Reflect on your most cherished visions and dreams.
What specific goals or aspirations have you been nurturing deep within your soul?

_____
_____
_____
_____
_____
_____
_____

How can you turn your cherished visions and dreams into actionable blueprints for your ultimate achievements? What initial steps can you take to move closer to realizing them?

_____
_____
_____
_____
_____
_____
_____
_____

#23

YOU CAN BECOME A WINNER ONLY IF YOU ARE WILLING TO WALK OVER THE EDGE

The concept of winning should never be equated with coming first – even if you're an elite sportsperson. Even if you come first, you can only really win if your position has required you to move over the edge of what you thought possible.

Only if your result has pushed beyond the limits of what is comfortable, both during the race and in preparation.

Winners are the ones who risk their reputation and everything they are to accomplish what they never thought they could.

#23 YOU CAN BECOME A WINNER ONLY IF YOU ARE WILLING TO WALK OVER THE EDGE

What is a recent situation where you stepped out of your comfort zone and took a risk, no matter how small?

What did you learn from that experience?

What are some potential benefits of taking calculated risks in your personal or professional life? How might it impact your mindset and performance?

Can you identify an area in your life where you've been avoiding risks due to fear or uncertainty? What is one small, manageable step you can take to begin embracing the unknown in that area?

What strategies or support can you put in place to manage and mitigate the potential downsides of taking risks?

#24

OUR ENERGY IS IN PROPORTION TO THE RESISTANCE IT MEETS

OK, doping allegations aside, we were once witness to the amounts of energy and strength one man can summon when he needs it. Yep, Floyd (Landis) met the resistance of his competitors and the terrain with unproportionable energy the day after "hitting the wall". (Tour de France 2006)

If we really want something, we develop the ability to summon ability, resources and energy to accomplish our dream. This is particularly true when what we want meets resistance. That's why a working mother can find the time to train for – and complete – an Ironman triathlon.

It's also why having a full life (as we all do) is never an excuse for not trying something new.

#24 OUR ENERGY IS IN PROPORTION TO THE RESISTANCE IT MEETS

Reflect on a recent challenge or obstacle you've encountered. How did overcoming this resistance impact your energy, motivation, or personal growth?

In what ways can you proactively seek out challenges or set higher goals to ensure your energy remains vibrant and growing?

#25

OTHER PEOPLE MAY NOT HAVE HAD HIGH EXPECTATIONS FOR ME... BUT I HAD HIGH EXPECTATIONS FOR MYSELF

SHANNON MILLER, OLYMPIC GYMNAST

Whose expectations do you fulfil?

Your's or those of others? It's a proven fact that your mind will move your body in the direction of your dominant thought, and obviously your thoughts can be influenced by what other people tell you. However the final decision lies with what you choose to believe.

Two fundamental rules govern choices: Firstly, you must know that every choice has a price. And, secondly, even when you haven't made a choice, you've made one! Get it?

Are your thoughts yours, or those of others?

What price are you willing to pay for not exercising a choice?

Mind Vitamins

#25 — OTHER PEOPLE MAY NOT HAVE HAD HIGH EXPECTATIONS FOR ME... BUT I HAD HIGH EXPECTATIONS FOR MYSELF

What negative self-beliefs or self-doubts may be hindering my performance, and how can I work on changing them?

_____
_____
_____
_____
_____
_____
_____
_____

How can I leverage self-belief to boost my motivation, resilience, and overall performance in challenging situations?

_____
_____
_____
_____
_____
_____
_____
_____

#26

OTHERS CAN STOP YOU TEMPORARILY – YOU ARE THE ONLY ONE WHO CAN DO IT PERMANENTLY

ZIG ZIGLAR

Think of a sporting hero who never tasted defeat. Or a leader who's alwaly successful. Or a team that achieves every goal.

If you can, let me know. Everybody has been stopped by others, but not one successful person has been stopped by themselves. They continue to push the boundaries, they continue to push themselves further, faster, longer.

Successful athletes (and people) explore the depths of their physiology and the depths of their psyche in order to move beyond their last performance.

Keep finding your barriers, then break them because others can deliver temporary setbacks, but only you can stop your efforts permanently.

Mind Vitamins

#26   OTHERS CAN STOP YOU TEMPORARILY - YOU ARE THE ONLY ONE WHO CAN DO IT PERMANENTLY

What negative self-beliefs or self-doubts may be hindering my performance, and how can I work on changing them?

_____
_____
_____
_____
_____
_____
_____

How can I leverage self-belief to boost my motivation, resilience, and overall performance in challenging situations?

_____
_____
_____
_____
_____
_____
_____
_____

#27

OUR BUSINESS IN LIFE IS NOT TO SUCCEED, BUT TO CONTINUE TO FAIL IN GOOD SPIRITS

ROBERT LOUIS STEVENSON

The great myth about performance is that of failing – or not getting what you want. We change this by focusing not on the result, but on the actions we took in order to achieve the result. You see, all results originate from actions, 90% of the things that happen to us happen because of decisions we've made.

Think of failure, or not getting the results you want, as the start of a process that will lead you to what you really want. To fail, is nothing more than your First Attempt At Learning. So the sooner you get back up from your pity-party, the sooner you'll be performing at your peak again.

073 Mind Vitamins

#27 OUR BUSINESS IN LIFE IS NOT TO SUCCEED, BUT TO CONTINUE TO FAIL IN GOOD SPIRITS

When was a time you faced failure with a positive attitude, and what did you learn from it?

_____
_____
_____
_____
_____
_____
_____
_____

How can you approach future challenges with a more resilient and optimistic mindset?

_____
_____
_____
_____
_____
_____
_____
_____

#28

OUT OF NEED SPRINGS DESIRE, AND OUT OF DESIRE SPRINGS THE ENERGY AND THE WILL TO WIN

DENIS WAITLEY

How badly do you want what you're training for, or working towards? My problem with most athletes — professional and amateur — is that they just don't want success badly enough.

A word that is often used, but seldom understood is Passion. When one looks at the origins of the word, the original Latin meaning of Passion is to suffer.

How many people are really willing to suffer for their results?

Get your hands on a photograph of Lance climbing to Luz Ardiden after his crash. That's a face of suffering. That's the picture of passion.

#28 OUT OF NEED SPRINGS DESIRE, AND OUT OF DESIRE SPRINGS THE ENERGY AND THE WILL TO WIN

What do you truly desire in your life or career, and how can you channel that desire into motivation?

_____
_____
_____
_____
_____
_____
_____
_____

How can you use your desires to fuel your efforts to achieve your goals?

_____
_____
_____
_____
_____
_____
_____
_____

#29

PAINT A MASTERPIECE DAILY. ALWAYS AUTOGRAPH YOUR WORK WITH EXCELLENCE

GREG HICKMAN

Have you ever given your brand a thought?

Top athletes spend time developing their brand – what sporting / racing characteristics they would like their competitors to associate them with.

Everyone has a "brand". How are you known in your company or in your team? What attributes do you have that people call on you for? How do you look? How do you make people feel?

Elite international tri-athlete Tim Don is associated with tenaciousness, Lance Armstrong with extreme discipline, BMW with sheer driving pleasure.

What do your competitors feel when they see you?

#29 PAINT A MASTERPIECE DAILY. ALWAYS AUTOGRAPH YOUR WORK WITH EXCELLENCE

How can you incorporate a commitment to excellence into your daily routine or work?

_____

What small, daily actions can you take to create a "masterpiece" in your life or profession?

#30

PARALYZE RESISTANCE WITH PERSISTENCE

WOODY HAYES

Even the biggest, hardest rock will crumble if hit often enough on the same spot for an appropriate amount of time. Your performance is exactly the same. Expect to find plateaus in your improvement.

The only way to move beyond this apparent resistance is to continue doing what you know to be right. Kids have a fantastic way of dealing with resistance – they keep working at Mom or Dad until they get what they want because they've (literally) worn Mom down. The same will happen with your performance if you keep at it.

Don't be like most South Africans and be as committed as a Kamikaze pilot on their 4th mission. Persist until you get where you want to be.

#30 PARALYZE RESISTANCE WITH PERSISTENCE

Can you recall a time when your persistence paid off despite facing resistance or obstacles?

_____
_____
_____
_____
_____
_____
_____

How can you apply this principle to your current challenges and goals?

_____
_____
_____
_____
_____
_____
_____
_____

3

CHAPTER 3

THE SECOND 30 DAYS

3

#31

YOU BECOME STRONG BY DEFYING DEFEAT AND BY TURNING LOSS INTO GAIN AND FAILURE TO SUCCESS

NAPOLEON

All success is preceded by pain, by loss, by defeat. If it's worth doing, and doing well, it's worth trying again. We learn so much more from defeat and failure than we ever do from victory or success.

You see, it's only in moments of defeat that we can choose to continue and every time we choose to continue, our resolve strengthens. We discover where to dig for extra – extra speed, extra endurance, extra guts.

You become stronger by continuing despite defeat.

#31 YOU BECOME STRONG BY DEFYING DEFEAT AND BY TURNING LOSS INTO GAIN AND FAILURE TO SUCCESS

Think of a past failure or loss – how did it contribute to your personal growth and future success?

_____
_____
_____
_____
_____
_____
_____
_____

How can you turn your current setbacks into stepping stones for a brighter future?

_____
_____
_____
_____
_____
_____
_____
_____

#32

YOU CAN DISCOVER MORE ABOUT A PERSON IN AN HOUR OF PLAY THAN IN A YEAR OF CONVERSATION

PLATO

There are only two ways in which to see beyond the masks people wear in their day-to-day life. One way is to play with them – like kids. The second is to compete with them in endurance sport.

You can also discover so much about yourself when you challenge yourself to something new – a longer distance, a new sport, a new racing partner.

Spend more time at play, it will reveal yourself and, when you approach training with the playful abandon of a five-year old, it will feel less like "work" and more like fun.

#32 YOU CAN DISCOVER MORE ABOUT A PERSON IN AN HOUR OF PLAY THAN IN A YEAR OF CONVERSATION

Reflect on a time when you connected with someone through play or leisure activities. What did you learn about them?

_____

How can you incorporate more play and leisure into your relationships to deepen your understanding of others?

_____

#33

GET UP AND GO, BUT DON'T FORGET YOUR SHOES

We so often get caught up in the excitement of the moment that we forget the truly important things. Excitement is good. It creates energy, motivation and movement. But it also creates haste, impatience and a propensity for mistakes. I've seen someone arrive at a bike race without their bike!

Find ways to temper your excitement, stretch it out over a period of time, and never take your eyes off the small stuff.

Small things like balance, family, and having a good time.

#33 GET UP AND GO, BUT DON'T FORGET YOUR SHOES

What essential preparations or details have you overlooked when pursuing your goals?

_____
_____
_____
_____
_____
_____
_____

How can you ensure you're fully equipped for your journey to success?

_____
_____
_____
_____
_____
_____
_____
_____

#34

PEOPLE RARELY SUCCEED, UNLESS THEY HAVE FUN IN WHAT THEY ARE DOING

DALE CARNEGIE

Haven't we all dreamt of doing something we really enjoy? We've been on long training rides dreaming that we could this everyday. We watch Ernie Els, thinking that he has a dream job.

Point is that there are lots of thing we love doing for fun. However, the moment you get paid to do anything, the moment there is a financial reward for your actions, those activities become work. The only way to keep fun in a routine, in work, is to continually find new challenges within the scope of what you do. Ernie Els for example tried to hone one particular part of his game in every tournament he played.

Having fun stimulates endorphins, these chemicals create movement, movement creates motivation.

#34 PEOPLE RARELY SUCCEED, UNLESS THEY HAVE FUN IN WHAT THEY ARE DOING

Are you currently enjoying what you're doing? If not, what changes can you make to inject more joy into your work?

How can you infuse elements of enjoyment and passion into your daily tasks and goals?

#35

HAPPINESS COMES WHEN YOUR WORK AND WORDS ARE OF BENEFIT TO YOURSELF AND OTHERS
BUDDHA

True fulfillment comes not from attaining your own goals. They are merely the catalyst. True happiness and fulfillment comes from sharing your knowledge, experience and wisdom with others.

Look beyond yourself in everything you do. Find opportunities to share what you have with others and I don't mean material stuff. There'll always be someone with less experience than you, someone who's been on a plateau longer than you, someone who could use advice, a shoulder, encouragement.

Besides, the best way to learn and to remember something is to share it and teach it to someone else. Try this – everyday.

You'll learn so much more!

#35 HAPPINESS COMES WHEN YOUR WORK AND WORDS ARE OF BENEFIT TO YOURSELF AND OTHERS

In what ways can your work and words be more beneficial to both yourself and those around you?

_____
_____
_____
_____
_____
_____
_____
_____
_____

How can you align your actions with the goal of creating happiness through positive contributions?

_____
_____
_____
_____
_____
_____
_____
_____

#36

TRY SOMETHING FRESH

I work with many athletes who start pre-season with loads of enthusiasm, lots of time on the road, great hopes for their goal events, and iron-clad training programmes and routines. And all goes well for the first eight weeks.

I see the same with new employees in business and on teams. Starting a new job always comes with a ton of enthusiasm

Then they get bored, frustrated, de-motivated, and predictable and their improvements plateau. By trying something fresh every six weeks you do yourself an enormous favour. You stimulate your muscles, you stimulate your thinking, you create fun, you get out of a rut.

The only difference between a rut and a grave is the depth. Create new stimuli often.

#36 TRY SOMETHING FRESH

Think about a recent situation where you stepped out of your comfort zone. What did you learn from that experience?

How can you regularly incorporate new and fresh approaches into your life or work to keep growing?

#37

THE SHORTEST WAY TO DO MANY THINGS IS TO DO ONLY ONE AT A TIME

Since school days our teachers, coaches and parent have told us to focus. But what is focus really?

Focus is a complete devotion to only one thing at a time. Being completely immersed in the moment – thinking of nothing else – for any appropriate amount of time.

To improve his batting, Jacques Kallis learnt to focus completely only when facing a bowler. In between deliveries, he adjusted his focus in order to "rest". This allowed him to bat for longer periods and score more runs.

Start training your focus at meal times. Don't eat in front of the TV, and focus completely on your meal, the taste, the texture – that's all. Try this for a few minutes and then progressively work at your focus for longer periods of time.

#37 THE SHORTEST WAY TO DO MANY THINGS IS TO DO ONLY ONE AT A TIME

How often do you find yourself multitasking? How might focusing on one task at a time improve your efficiency and effectiveness?

What strategies can you implement to prioritize and tackle tasks one at a time for better results?

#38

A GREAT MORNING STARTS WITH A GOOD NIGHT

Motivation is often confused with keeping busy, keeping a hectic schedule and getting more done than others.

Athletes, in particular, try to motivate themselves by doing more, going further, and training harder than their competitors.

The fact is that rest is equally, if not more, important than training to keep motivation up and to see constant improvement in results. Not only is a good night's sleep essential, but active rest should also form a major part of your life. Take regular mini-breaks through out the year as opposed to only one long holiday.

Take regular breaks in your training – one rest day per week at least. And, finally, make sure that you develop the correct periodisation roster, in your work, you training and in your play.

#38 A GREAT MORNING STARTS WITH A GOOD NIGHT

How can you improve your night-time routines to ensure a better start to your mornings?

What habits or practices can you adopt to optimize your sleep and create a positive morning routine?

#39

THE FUTURE DEPENDS ON WHAT WE DO IN THE PRESENT

GHANDI

It's great to have a plan. It's great to have goals. It's fantastic when your plan leads to your goals and you actually achieve them. Problem is that most people are great waiters.

Young people on my seminars tell me, "One day I will … (run Comrades / Buy the sports car / Climb Kili…)". Older people on my seminars tell me, "If only I had … (run Comrades / Bought the sports car / Climbed Kili…)" So my only conclusion is that NOTHING happens between the ages 25 and 55!

Make sure you do something deliberate every day that will move you towards your goals. Take massive action everyday. Movement creates motivation.

Never leave the location where you set a goal without taking action towards it. The future begins now!!

#39 THE FUTURE DEPENDS ON WHAT WE DO IN THE PRESENT

What actions are you taking today to build the future you desire?

_____
_____
_____
_____
_____
_____
_____

How can you ensure that your present actions align with your long-term goals and aspirations?

_____
_____
_____
_____
_____
_____
_____
_____
_____
_____
_____

#40

IF YOU REFUSE TO ACCEPT ANYTHING BUT THE BEST YOU OFTEN GET IT

Most people are push-overs! We seem to accept everything we get given – even when we're not very happy with it!

Have you ever complained when your steak was not done exactly the way you ordered it? Stop accepting what you get.

It's a fact of life that you get what you deserve – both good and bad. But if you refuse to accept indifference from your coach, your training partners, your customers, your suppliers – you'll stop getting mediocrity.

Similarly, if you become determined to get the best results you can get – you'll get them the moment you refuse to settle for anything less. Of course this normally means having to sacrifice something else, like the extra helping of desert!

#40 IF YOU REFUSE TO ACCEPT ANYTHING BUT THE BEST YOU OFTEN GET IT

Do you often settle for less than your best effort or results? How might this quote inspire you to aim higher?

_____
_____
_____
_____
_____
_____
_____
_____

What strategies can you use to consistently strive for and achieve the best in your endeavors?

_____
_____
_____
_____
_____
_____
_____
_____

#41

YOU CAN HAVE ANYTHING YOU WANT, IF YOU WANT IT BADLY ENOUGH. YOU CAN BE ANYTHING YOU WANT TO BE, DO ANYTHING YOU SET OUT TO ACCOMPLISH IF YOU HOLD TO THAT DESIRE WITH SINGLENESS OF PURPOSE

ABRAHAM LINCOLN

Singleness of purpose = Laser-like Focus. And that's the biggest challenge facing amateur athletes and multi-sport enthusiasts. We try to balance work and sport, and canoeing, cycling, running, surf-skiing, MTB'ing – the list goes on.

In life you largely get what you focus on. My wife recently wanted to buy a new car. She wanted a soft-top convertible, and once she decided on a make and model, she suddenly started seeing them everywhere. So much for wanting to be different!

Of course the number of those vehicles on the road hadn't suddenly increased. Her awareness just increased. Singleness of purpose increases awareness and that increases accomplishment.

#41

YOU CAN HAVE ANYTHING YOU WANT, IF YOU WANT IT BADLY ENOUGH. YOU CAN BE ANYTHING YOU WANT TO BE, DO ANYTHING YOU SET OUT TO ACCOMPLISH IF YOU HOLD TO THAT DESIRE WITH SINGLENESS OF PURPOSE

What is your most burning desire or goal, and how can you strengthen your commitment to it?

_____
_____
_____
_____
_____
_____
_____

How can you maintain a strong and unwavering focus on your aspirations?

_____
_____
_____
_____
_____
_____
_____
_____

#42

YOU CAN STAND TALL WITHOUT STANDING ON SOMEONE. YOU CAN BE A VICTOR WITHOUT HAVING VICTIMS

Very often victory is defined by beating others. Surely if you want to be #1 you have to get there first. But if you manage to do this without causing emotional hurt to others you become a true victor.

Bruce Fordyce relates the story of his famous victory passes during the last 10km's of 9 Comrades victories. He says that as he passed the leading athlete, he'd say to them, "You're running like a star."

On the surface this seems like a compliment, but the mental impact of this is far greater than the traditional "sledging" or insults. If I'm running like a star, and Fordyce comes past me like I'm looking for parking, how must he running?

You'll remember of course that Bruce never lost the lead once he took it!!

#42 YOU CAN STAND TALL WITHOUT STANDING ON SOMEONE. YOU CAN BE A VICTOR WITHOUT HAVING VICTIMS

Reflect on your leadership style. Are you lifting others up or stepping on them to succeed? How can you ensure your success doesn't come at the expense of others?

_____
_____
_____
_____
_____
_____
_____
_____

How can you achieve victory without creating victims in your path to success?

_____
_____
_____
_____
_____
_____
_____
_____

#43

YOU CANNOT CONSISTENTLY PERFORM IN A MANNER WHICH IS INCONSISTENT WITH THE WAY YOU SEE YOURSELF

ZIG ZIGLAR

I've written about presence previously, but we cannot ignore the fact that your actions result from your thoughts – not the other way around.

When you see yourself as an accomplished athlete that is what you will be.

Several years ago I thought it would be great to ply my trade as a Speaker and Trainer internationally. So I did. Without any previous experience, I started seeing myself as an international speaker, I applied that to my marketing material and to everything I did. It wasn't long before the business I craved started coming into my office. 25 years later and I'm still at it!

Find out what defines you as an athlete, as a person, as a businessman. Once you know this, and you know what defines successful people in your chosen field, you just need to model their views of the world.

#43 YOU CANNOT CONSISTENTLY PERFORM IN A MANNER WHICH IS INCONSISTENT WITH THE WAY YOU SEE YOURSELF

How do you perceive yourself, and does this self-image align with your goals and ambitions?

_____
_____
_____
_____
_____
_____
_____

What steps can you take to develop a self-image that empowers you to perform consistently at your best?

_____
_____
_____
_____
_____
_____
_____
_____

#44

YOU CAN'T CHANGE THE WIND, YOU CAN HOWEVER ADJUST YOUR SAILS

There are some things in life you can control, and lots of things you can't. I remember the inaugural Totalsports Challenge – a 7 discipline endurance event.

They allowed 20 individual entries and I was one of them. Work pressure forced me to only fly down the afternoon before the event. I borrowed a surf-ski and a MTB because the airline would only let me travel with one bike.

We woke up on race day with the wind howling. All these things I couldn't control. I just had to adjust the way I tackled the race. Unfortunately a crash on the unfamiliar MTB (the bike, not the route) ended my race.

Remember, you control your attitude through your thought-processes. Focus on what you can control and never forget that circumstances can only affect your results if you allow them to.

#44 YOU CAN'T CHANGE THE WIND, YOU CAN HOWEVER ADJUST YOUR SAILS

What circumstances or challenges are beyond your control at the moment? How can you adapt your approach to navigate them effectively?

___

How can you become more flexible and adaptable in the face of changing winds in your life or career?

___

#45

YOU CAN'T GET MUCH DONE IN LIFE IF YOU ONLY WORK ON THE DAYS WHEN YOU FEEL GOOD

If there's one thing I can guarantee in life, in business and in sport it's that you'll have days from hell. Days when you get out of bed and you know it's going to be a disaster.

There are only two reasons for this. One, you expect it and so your mind will move your body in that direction. Two, the paw-paw really does hit the proverbial and you don't deal with it resourcefully.

So what's the secret?

Push through it. Ask yourself, "in what ways can I make the most of this?" Feel the discomfort and do it anyway. I've had some of my most remarkable training sessions, both in terms of quality and perceived exertion after I had to force myself to do it.

In business I've also delivered some outstanding work after not being "in the zone" at the start.

#45 YOU CAN'T GET MUCH DONE IN LIFE IF YOU ONLY WORK ON THE DAYS WHEN YOU FEEL GOOD

Reflect on a time when you pushed through a difficult day and achieved something significant. What motivated you?

How can you cultivate discipline and consistency, even on days when you don't feel your best?

#46

DO NOT CONFUSE MOTION AND PROGRESS. A ROCKING HORSE KEEPS MOVING BUT DOES NOT MAKE ANY PROGRESS

I see many people who start projects with great enthusiasm. They rush and get the latest advice, the best equipment; they spend every cent they can afford to. Then they move – constantly. They're busy – constantly. But the most important question is whether or not their actions lead them to their goals.

If your actions do not lead you directly to your goals, they are wasted efforts. These result only in motion, not progress. Before you start, map out your route to your goal. Create specific actions that will meet the milestones on the road to your goal.

Make actions count.

#46 DO NOT CONFUSE MOTION AND PROGRESS. A ROCKING HORSE KEEPS MOVING BUT DOES NOT MAKE ANY PROGRESS

Are you often busy but not making significant progress? How can you ensure that your actions lead to meaningful results?

What can you do to distinguish between motion and progress in your personal and professional life?

#47

YOU NEVER WILL BE THE PERSON YOU CAN BE IF PRESSURE, TENSION AND DISCIPLINE ARE TAKEN OUT OF YOUR LIFE

Every decision you've ever made has come down to only one question. "Will I experience pleasure or pain?"

Most people will try to avoid pain and actively seek out pleasure. However, as we mature, we develop an understanding of a concept called Delayed Gratification. This implies that we understand that discomfort litters the road to success and pleasure.

Ultimately it is only discomfort that moves us to action. We train smarter and harder, we eat better, we buy better equipment because our last race, or our position created more discomfort than pleasure.

We also make better work and business decisions - but only once we deal with the bad decisions!

#47 YOU NEVER WILL BE THE PERSON YOU CAN BE IF PRESSURE, TENSION AND DISCIPLINE ARE TAKEN OUT OF YOUR LIFE

How have pressure and discipline helped shape your character and capabilities?

_____

How can you embrace and utilize pressure, tension, and discipline as catalysts for personal growth and success?

_____

#48

WHEN THE WILL IS READY THE FEET ARE LIGHT

Ever find yourself in a struggle to get moving?

Your body says, "You need to train." But your mind won't listen, or finds a number of excuses not to. It's because your motivation is focused on the wrong part of your psyche.

Your mind moves your body – not the other way around. So if you want to get motivated to train or to enter the next event, find a compelling mental reason to do so. Similarly, when racing, attack the event mentally first through visualisation exercises.

Your mind cannot distinguish between reality and imagination. And your imagination always wins!

#48 WHEN THE WILL IS READY THE FEET ARE LIGHT

Think about a time when your strong determination led to effortless action. What was the goal, and how did you stay motivated?

How can you strengthen your willpower to make your actions feel more effortless in pursuing your objectives?

#49

TAKE OFF THE BLINDERS. YOU HAVE TO SEE OPPORTUNITY BEFORE YOU CAN SEIZE IT

This applies to both the mental and physical aspects of performance. More often than not though, familiarity leads to lack of vision. We're told that it takes 21 days to form a habit. But you need to constantly change the way you do things.

You become mentally stale when you put on the blinkers and just do things the way you've always done them. You need to create a compelling vision of your performance when you set off. "See" your race time, "see" the results you want. Even if they don't happen immediately, research shows that your body will be moved in the direction of your subconscious.

As a kid, I always drove past an area thinking that I would love to live there one day. Of course I forgot about these thoughts, but guess what – I lived there for almost 10 years!

There are opportunities everywhere – you just need to go out and look for them!

#49 TAKE OFF THE BLINDERS. YOU HAVE TO SEE OPPORTUNITY BEFORE YOU CAN SEIZE IT

Are there opportunities in your life or career that you might be overlooking? How can you become more attentive to potential opportunities?

_____
_____
_____
_____
_____
_____
_____
_____

How can you proactively prepare to seize opportunities when they arise?

_____
_____
_____
_____
_____
_____
_____

#50

THE BEST AND FASTEST WAY TO LEARN A SPORT IS TO WATCH AND IMITATE A CHAMPION

Every result comes about from the actions you take on the way to that result. Because we live in a world of cause and effect (as proven by Isaac Newton) we will find that similar actions produce similar results. Every top sportsperson or successful businessman will tell you about their idols, people in their area of performance that they looked up to and emulated when they started out. Do what they do. Don't re-write the book.

Early in my cycling career it was Greg Lemond – winner of the Tour de France by the narrowest margin in history; 8 seconds. At that stage I was also co-ordinating training rides for schoolboys. One day a skinny youngster with knock-knees and big feet came along wearing tennis shoes. It was only a 40km ride but he suffered. I nursed him home after dark, not thinking we'll see him again. But he came back.

His name, Jacques Fullard, twice South African Elite Road Race champion.

#50 THE BEST AND FASTEST WAY TO LEARN A SPORT IS TO WATCH AND IMITATE A CHAMPION

How can you apply the principle of watching and learning from champions to your own personal or professional development?

_____
_____
_____
_____
_____
_____
_____
_____
_____
_____

Who are the "champions" in your field or area of interest that you can study and emulate?

_____
_____
_____
_____
_____
_____
_____
_____

#51

THE COUNTRY IS FULL OF GOOD COACHES. WHAT IT TAKES TO WIN IS A BUNCH OF INTERESTED PLAYERS

DON CORYELL, EX-SAN DIEGO CHARGERS COACH

Whether you participate in a team sport or not; whether you work alone or as part of a team, the most important thing for performance is involvement and interest. Of course I'm not saying you don't need a good coach – you do; but the coach cannot motivate you!

Coaches, managers, fans, all those external sources of "motivation" are really just activators. They activate you. They drive you. They influence what you are motivated to do. Ultimately motivation comes from within you. You choose what you do and when. You make the choice between the lavish breakfast and the training ride.

Your challenge is to find interest and maintain it. How do you that? Get out of your routine, try new training programmes, enter new events. That's the bonus of multi-sport – there are so many disciplines you can choose between them!

#51 THE COUNTRY IS FULL OF GOOD COACHES. WHAT IT TAKES TO WIN IS A BUNCH OF INTERESTED PLAYERS

Reflect on your role as a leader or coach. How can you inspire and maintain the interest and commitment of those you lead or coach?

How can you create a team of enthusiastic and engaged individuals dedicated to a common goal?

#52

GREAT WORKS ARE PERFORMED NOT BY STRENGTH BUT BY PERSEVERANCE

When a colonel retired from active duty, he started cooking for his wife at home. She remarked that the chicken he prepared every Tuesday was delicious, and that maybe he could sell the recipe for some extra money. After going to over 400 restaurants, the Colonel continued his quest.

He eventually knocked on the door of a guy named Frank Maguire. Frank didn't want to buy the recipe either, but offered the Colonel $20 000-00 to start his own restaurant. On two conditions. Frank wanted 20% of the profits, and secondly, he wanted to name the new eating place.

In 1985 Kentucky Fried Chicken was sold to Pepsico for $250 million. (You do the math!)

Your sport and life activities are the same. Perseverance is consistently ranked as one of the top leadership and success qualities. How easily do you give up?

#52 GREAT WORKS ARE PERFORMED NOT BY STRENGTH BUT BY PERSEVERANCE

Think of a challenging project or goal you've accomplished through perseverance. What kept you going?

_____
_____
_____
_____
_____
_____

How can you develop and maintain the perseverance needed to achieve great works in the future?

_____
_____
_____
_____
_____
_____
_____
_____

#53

HARD WORK SPOTLIGHTS THE CHARACTER OF PEOPLE: SOME TURN UP THEIR SLEEVES, SOME TURN UP THEIR NOSES, AND SOME DON'T TURN UP AT ALL

Average people and average athletes crumble at the thought of hard work. Most of us are prepared to do enough to stay in the pack. Very few are prepared to go beyond the masses.

I remember an old song… "When the going gets tough…" and its true – only the "tough get going". The rest leave or don't show up at all. Super athletes, from Lance to Tiger, from Mike Horn to Alex Harris, have the ability to turn up when the hardest work is required.

…And you? Do you suffer "excusitis"? Looking for every reason why you shouldn't? Every reason why you can't? Or do you look for slightest possibility that something will work and succeed and then you tackle it with everything you have? Are you a pessimist or an optimist?

(By the way, a study has found that optimists live longer! Are you in?)

#53 HARD WORK SPOTLIGHTS THE CHARACTER OF PEOPLE: SOME TURN UP THEIR SLEEVES, SOME TURN UP THEIR NOSES, AND SOME DON'T TURN UP AT ALL

In your experience, how has hard work revealed the character of individuals around you?

___

How can you ensure that hard work spotlights your character in a positive way, inspiring others and achieving your goals?

___

#54

YOU MUST REMAIN FOCUSED ON YOUR JOURNEY TO GREATNESS

LES BROWN

This is probably the toughest challenge of a multi-sport enthusiast or a very talented person. You know, those people who seem to excel at everything they do. Success comes to those who focus all their energy on one goal.

Were you one of those kids that became an unashamed sadomasochist when given a magnifying glass? You remember? Positioning the magnifying glass so as to concentrate the sunlight on the head of a pin in order to torture and kill as many ants as possible? That's focus - concentrating all your energy on one thing!!

Focus creates energy. Focus creates purpose. Focus creates movement. Focus creates relationships with like-minded people. Focus delivers results!

#54 YOU MUST REMAIN FOCUSED ON YOUR JOURNEY TO GREATNESS

What is your vision of greatness, and how can you stay committed to that journey even in the face of challenges?

How can you maintain unwavering focus on your path to achieving greatness in your life or profession?

#55

DESTINY IS NOT A MATTER OF CHANCE, IT IS A MATTER OF CHOICE; IT IS NOT A THING TO BE WAITED FOR, IT IS A THING TO BE ACHIEVED

WILLIAM JENNINGS BRYAN

Hands up if you believe in destiny, in chance, in luck, in co-incidence? Studies show that people who achieve the goals they set for themselves do not! Understand that "destiny" is not the result of a series of random happenings. Was it Dricus' destiny to win the World Champs? Was it the Springboks' destiny to win 2 RWC Championships in a row? No.

"Destiny" is a choice. Success is a choice. Think of all the choices you made in life – or failed to make in life – that have led you to be reading this. If you took just one different option, if you had made only one different choice your life today would not be exactly as it is now. You can look at this from two perspectives. If you're happy with your life as it is now, you'll say you made the right choices. If you're suffering discontent in your current situation, you'll most likely be blaming "destiny" and refuse to accept that it was the choices you've made up till now.

Be in control. Appoint yourself as your life manager and start making choices instead of suffering the fate of "chance".

#55 DESTINY IS NOT A MATTER OF CHANCE, IT IS A MATTER OF CHOICE; IT IS NOT A THING TO BE WAITED FOR, IT IS A THING TO BE ACHIEVED

How can you make choices that shape your destiny rather than leaving it to chance?

#56

TRUE SUCCESS IS ALWAYS PRECEDED BY DISCOMFORT

Anything worth achieving is worth suffering for! I'm sure people have asked you what you are passionate about, and you've probably replied your sport, work, your spouse, maybe your car/bike.

Before you answer that question again, I'd like to remind you of the origin of the word "passion". In its original Latin derivative, passion means literally "to suffer for". As in "The Passion of the Christ". This really means the "the suffering of the Christ". Thus, what you are stating when you say you are passionate about something is that you would be willing to suffer for it. Suffering equals discomfort.

The journey to what you really want to achieve is littered with discomfort and suffering. Think back to any gift you got as a kid that you didn't have to work for. What happened to it? Isn't it true that you attach more value to something you have suffered for than to something that merely fell into your lap?

#56 TRUE SUCCESS IS ALWAYS PRECEDED BY DISCOMFORT

Think of a time when you experienced discomfort on your path to success. How did it contribute to your achievements?

How can you embrace discomfort as a necessary step toward true success in the future?

#57

TRUE GREATNESS IS OFTEN REVEALED THROUGH ABSOLUTE SIMPLICITY

Try this training technique. But let me warn you, it's revolutionary! Are you ready for it? Here it is…

Get on your bike, in your kayak, on the road and spend time there. The same with your mind management techniques – just start practicing them. True greatness is the result of doing the basics right – nothing more. Lance scouted the climbs in spring, Tiger started with putting, my 9 year-old twins develop a love for activity not by "training" but by simply being active. With their dad, of course.

The greatest inventions are also based on simplicity and there are too many to name here. When in doubt, distill what it is you want to do right down to its basic elements. Do them well and you'll do well.

I lie.

You'll excel.

#57 TRUE GREATNESS IS OFTEN REVEALED THROUGH ABSOLUTE SIMPLICITY

How can you simplify your goals or approach to reveal your true greatness?

What steps can you take to remove unnecessary complexity and distractions from your path to greatness?

#58

JUST BECAUSE YOU DESERVE IT DOESN'T MEAN THAT YOU'RE GOING TO GET IT. SOMETIMES YOU'VE GOT TO TAKE WHAT'S YOURS

I find this to be an alarming trend in the world today.

People seem to think they deserve things just because of who they are (or think they are) or because of what they've done. Of course you often feel that, because you've put in the hours, you deserve the result. Accept the fact that life is not always fair, and that the real world does not protect you from failure, loss, defeat, and other negative things school tried to shield you from.

In life there are winners and losers, there are those who have and those who don't have. Don't just deserve things – go out and claim them. Take them for yourself (legally of course)!

#58 JUST BECAUSE YOU DESERVE IT DOESN'T MEAN THAT YOU'RE GOING TO GET IT. SOMETIMES YOU'VE GOT TO TAKE WHAT'S YOURS

Reflect on a situation where you felt you deserved something but had to take action to attain it. What did you learn from that experience?

_____

How can you proactively work to claim what you believe you deserve in your life or career?

_____

#59

EVERYONE WHO GOT WHERE HE IS HAS HAD TO BEGIN WHERE HE WAS
ROBERT LOUIS STEVENSON

What we never see when we admire the achievements of top sports stars, businesspeople, and even occasionally celebrities, is the hard work and dedication that goes on behind the scenes.

No matter what it is you want to accomplish, you cannot deny your starting point. And that's where you should focus when you start. Not on your goal, but on what you have now. You need to use what you have now, build on it, grow it, develop it.

Richard Branson started in his parents' basement and built an empire which now consists of 265 companies. But he didn't start with this in mind. Look at Mondi Zondeki, the paddler from the Valley of 1000 Hills. As a youngster he watched the Duzi Canoe race and, with no background in paddling he has achieved remarkable placings.

#59 EVERYONE WHO GOT WHERE HE IS HAS HAD TO BEGIN WHERE HE WAS

How can you embrace your current starting point as the foundation for your future success?

What actions can you take to progress from where you are now toward your desired destination?

#60

THE GEM CANNOT BE POLISHED WITHOUT FRICTION, NOR MAN PERFECTED WITHOUT TRIALS
CHINESE PROVERB

Sport is not easy. Life is not easy. Deal with it.

Diamonds become diamonds through extreme heat and pressure, and after all that they look rather ubiquitous when they are first mined. Then they get cut and polished before they look anything like the object you've sacrificed your new TT bike for to keep your missus happy.

Embrace suffering in training and in events. Embrace trials in life because it is these moments of discomfort and friction that shape and polish the person and athlete that you are becoming.

#60 THE GEM CANNOT BE POLISHED WITHOUT FRICTION, NOR MAN PERFECTED WITHOUT TRIALS

Think of a trial or challenge that has refined your character. How did you emerge stronger?

_____
_____
_____
_____
_____
_____
_____

How can you view future trials as opportunities for personal growth and self-improvement?

_____
_____
_____
_____
_____
_____
_____

4

CHAPTER 4

THE THIRD 30 DAYS

4

#61

THE FIRST REQUISITE OF SUCCESS IS THE ABILITY TO APPLY YOUR PHYSICAL AND MENTAL ENERGIES TO ONE PROBLEM WITHOUT GROWING WEARY

THOMAS EDISON

The problem with modern society is that so many people demand our attention so frequently. Thus we find ourselves fragmented between various people, issues and projects. I know, it'll be an ideal world (of sponsorship probably) for us to focus only on our sport, but we'll only perform to our true potential at anything once we have learnt to apply total focus to one thing at a time.

Try this exercise to help you build your concentration span. At your next meal, clear your mind of everything before you start eating. Now, for the duration of the meal focus only on your meal. Think about the taste of the food, its texture, its colour, your enjoyment of it – whatever – just remain focused on your meal. Don't watch TV, don't shout at the kids, don't discuss philosophy, and don't worry about the animal that gave its life for your piece of steak.

Chances are you'll find this difficult. If you can't do this for 10 minutes, how do you think you'll manage to focus during a 4 hour endurance sport event? Or a day at the office.

#61 THE FIRST REQUISITE OF SUCCESS IS THE ABILITY TO APPLY YOUR PHYSICAL AND MENTAL ENERGIES TO ONE PROBLEM WITHOUT GROWING WEARY

How can you develop your ability to maintain focus and energy on a single problem until it's resolved?

What strategies can you implement to prevent burnout and stay committed to solving important challenges?

#62

GREAT THINGS ARE NOT DONE BY IMPULSE, BUT BY A SERIES OF SMALL THINGS BROUGHT TOGETHER

VINCENT VAN GOGH

If you've ever done something (like a half-marathon or more) on impulse you'll know this. When I was studying a girl who studied with us thought she'd join us for one (a 21km run) – "just for fun". Well she arrived at the finish after we'd finished the beers and the "FINISH" banner had been taken down.

Training is the same. Don't do in training what you'll be doing in the race. Successful racing is the culmination of great periodisation and a series of small measured efforts during training. All these efforts add up through "training effect" to deliver great things when put together t the right time.

Be sure therefore that you don't waste energy on things that will not take you toward your goal. Contador forgot this when he tried to "break" Rasmussen to the summit of the Col d' Aubisque. He lost 35 seconds.

#62 GREAT THINGS ARE NOT DONE BY IMPULSE, BUT BY A SERIES OF SMALL THINGS BROUGHT TOGETHER

Reflect on a significant achievement that resulted from a series of small actions. What was the journey like?

_____
_____
_____
_____
_____
_____
_____

How can you break down your larger goals into smaller, manageable tasks to make progress?

_____
_____
_____
_____
_____
_____
_____

#63

ABILITY IS WHAT YOU'RE CAPABLE OF DOING. MOTIVATION DETERMINES WHAT YOU DO. ATTITUDE DETERMINES HOW WELL YOU DO IT
LOU HOTLZ

Why do so few South Africans perform on the world sport stage? Why is it that, whenever there's a world cup on the horizon, we shoot ourselves and our athletes in the foot? See the problem isn't ability, or motivation. The issue is Attitude.

We've all heard about the effect of attitude, but let me put it bluntly. Every action begins with a thought (this activates your ability). Every action requires a motivation (a reason for doing it). And if every action begins with a thought, then it is your thought-processes that define your attitude. Whose attitude is it? Yours. Who controls it? You do.

Therefore, you choose your results. Simple, isn't it. No go practice.

#63 ABILITY IS WHAT YOU'RE CAPABLE OF DOING. MOTIVATION DETERMINES WHAT YOU DO. ATTITUDE DETERMINES HOW WELL YOU DO IT

How can you leverage your abilities by enhancing your motivation and attitude toward your goals?

_____
_____
_____
_____
_____
_____
_____
_____

What steps can you take to improve your motivation and cultivate a positive attitude for greater success?

_____
_____
_____
_____
_____
_____
_____
_____

#64

I AM A LUCKY MAN

CHRISTOPHER REEVE

The single biggest problem I find with motivation is that when people are demotivated, they focus externally. They lament about everything they haven't got, and everything that other people, both their colleagues and competitors have got. They blame their environment, their equipment. Of course they never blame their attitude.

Great performers have the ability to look inward when they are challenged. The focus on the things they do have, and they play to their strengths.

Christopher Reeve (the original Superman) was paralysed from the neck down, couldn't breathe without a ventilator, and yet he found things to be thankful for. That's why he was a "lucky man"

How lucky are you?

#64

I AM A LUCKY MAN

What are you grateful for in your life, and how can you remind yourself of your blessings regularly?

_____
_____
_____
_____
_____
_____
_____
_____
_____
_____
_____
_____
_____
_____
_____
_____
_____

#65

YOU CAN'T CROSS THE SEA MERELY BY STANDING AND STARING AT THE WATER

RABINDRANATH TAGORE

While it can be inspiring to watch events on TV and even live at the venue, merely watching won't get you any closer to completing an event. But don't negate the value of attending events prior to competing in them.

Getting a feel for multi-sport, endurance events and anything "new" is often helpful. Not only will experience the effort required first-hand, you'll also get to meet some of the athletes, chat to them and gain from their experience.

Do the same in business. Find a mentor or research the area of specialisation you want to be an expert on.

The easiest (and cheapest) way to learn is usually from other people's mistakes!

#65 YOU CAN'T CROSS THE SEA MERELY BY STANDING AND STARING AT THE WATER

Think about a goal or dream that you've been hesitant to pursue. How can you take the first steps to cross your metaphorical sea?

_____
_____
_____
_____
_____
_____
_____

How can you overcome hesitations and fears to move forward in pursuit of your ambitions?

_____
_____
_____
_____
_____
_____
_____

#66

CONCENTRATION IS THE ABILITY TO THINK ABOUT ABSOLUTELY NOTHING WHEN IT IS ABSOLUTELY NECESSARY

RAY KNIGHT

The most important gift you can give yourself is a clear mind.

In order to perform well, stay on single track, stay upright in washing surf, you need to focus and concentrate.

You can't do this if your mind is cluttered.

Mind clutter makes concentration difficult and your little inner voice is so powerful it can "talk" to you at about 400 words per minute. Problem is you can only comprehend around 180 words per minute.

Clear the static, get tuned in to the right frequency, and you'll hear what you need to hear from your powerful inner voice.

#66 CONCENTRATION IS THE ABILITY TO THINK ABOUT ABSOLUTELY NOTHING WHEN IT IS ABSOLUTELY NECESSARY

Are you often distracted when you need to concentrate? How can you improve your ability to focus when it's crucial?

_____
_____
_____
_____
_____
_____

What strategies can you use to enhance your concentration skills in demanding situations?

_____
_____
_____
_____
_____
_____
_____
_____

#67

DEFEAT IS NOT THE WORST OF FAILURES. NOT TO HAVE TRIED IS THE TRUE FAILURE

GEORGE E. WOODBERRY

You are only defeated when you don't get up again and try again. Life would be boring indeed if we succeeded at everything we tried. In research I did many years ago, I measured the feeling of accomplishment varsity students experienced during adventure activities.

The result was that the experience was more intense when the participant had a higher degree of control over the outcome and if there was a risk of failure!

After all, to fail is merely your First Attempt In Learning. You only truly fail when you remain in the cocoon of your comfort zone; never try anything new and never risking anything!

#67 DEFEAT IS NOT THE WORST OF FAILURES. NOT TO HAVE TRIED IS THE TRUE FAILURE

Recall a time when you hesitated to try something and later regretted it. How can you overcome the fear of failure in the future?

_____
_____
_____
_____
_____
_____
_____

What can you do to adopt a mindset where trying, even if it leads to defeat, is seen as a valuable learning experience?

_____
_____
_____
_____
_____
_____
_____
_____

#68

DISCIPLINE AND CONCENTRATION ARE A MATTER OF BEING INTERESTED

TOM KITE

Have you ever sat through a boring movie? (When it's your better half's birthday and they chose the movie it doesn't count). When you are not "into" something, when it doesn't hold you in awe, it's difficult to concentrate on it.

The pre-requisite of focus and concentration is interest. Interest in your performance, interest in training methods, interest in the inner workings of your equipment. This is why new equipment is such a good motivator. You suddenly become interested again in your sport – the same way you increase your desire to train and compete when you enter for a new event.

At the end of the day, the biggest difference between amateur and elite athletes is not just ability, rather its discipline and consistency in preparation.

#68 DISCIPLINE AND CONCENTRATION ARE A MATTER OF BEING INTERESTED

How can you cultivate a genuine interest in your tasks or goals to enhance your discipline and concentration?

_____
_____
_____
_____
_____
_____
_____
_____

What methods can you employ to maintain focus and discipline when working on activities that may not naturally captivate your interest?

_____
_____
_____
_____
_____
_____
_____

#69

YOU WIN SOME, YOU LOSE SOME, YOU WRECK SOME

DALE EARNHARDT

When things go well, who gets the credit? When things go badly, who gets the blame? If you're like most people, everyone gets the blame for the latter. Everyone from competitors, coaches, event organisers, equipment – even the weather! Or in the case of business, management and the team that you're part of. Or the customer.

Accept the fact that you will not achieve the results you want all the time. Sometimes you will lose, and sometimes you will win. Sometimes you'll become the "victim" of things that appear beyond your control. But most of the time you are responsible for what happens to you – whether you like it or not.

Top athletes accept responsibility for both good and bad results – unlike the Proteas! You create the conditions that lead to upwards of 85% of things that happen to you through your focus, mental approach and physical preparation.

#69 YOU WIN SOME, YOU LOSE SOME, YOU WRECK SOME

Can you think of a recent experience where you faced success, failure, or a setback? How did you handle each of these situations?

_____
_____
_____
_____
_____
_____
_____
_____

How can you turn your losses into opportunities for growth and success?

_____
_____
_____
_____
_____
_____
_____

#70

YOUR GOALS, MINUS YOUR DOUBTS, EQUAL YOUR REALITY

The reason I believe so many adults fail to convert the majority of their goals into reality is that they succumb to their doubts. Our kids set goals. You did when you were a kid – and you realised a high percentage of them. Much higher than you do now.

The difference? Kids refuse to relinquish their dreams (goals) to doubts. As we get older we ask far too many "What If?" questions. We become victims of our own fear.

We get blinded by our own imperfections. We focus on our weaknesses instead of our strengths. Many years ago someone told me that I have strengths and weaknesses and that I should work on my weaknesses. I did, and I ended up with strong weaknesses!!

Look for reasons that you will succeed, rather than for reasons you won't. Minimise your doubts and increase the measure of your reality.

#70 YOUR GOALS, MINUS YOUR DOUBTS, EQUAL YOUR REALITY

What doubts are holding you back from achieving your goals?

_____
_____
_____
_____
_____
_____
_____
_____

How can you overcome these doubts to make your goals a reality?

_____
_____
_____
_____
_____
_____
_____

#71

YOUR PAST IS NOT YOUR POTENTIAL. IN ANY HOUR YOU CAN CHOOSE TO LIBERATE THE FUTURE

Remember the movie "Groundhog Day"? That's when Bill Murray's character wakes up every morning and experiences the same day over and over again. His past equaled his future. Everything that happened to him yesterday happens to him again today. His life is utterly predictable.

Fortunately our lives, endeavours and results aren't. The past does not equal the future, and everything you have already accomplished by the very nature that you have accomplished it once, means that you can do it again.

Further, if we've done something once, it means that we can not only replicate that performance, but we can also improve on it. You choose what you will become in the future.

The problem with this choice though, is that if you fail to make a conscious choice, you've made one.

#71 YOUR PAST IS NOT YOUR POTENTIAL. IN ANY HOUR YOU CAN CHOOSE TO LIBERATE THE FUTURE

Reflect on a past mistake or setback. How can you use it to fuel your future success?

_____
_____
_____
_____
_____
_____
_____

What action can you take right now to move towards your potential and a brighter future?

_____
_____
_____
_____
_____
_____
_____

#72

YOU'RE NEVER BEATEN UNTIL YOU ADMIT IT

GEORGE S PATTON

When the British sprinter John Regis lined up at a Grand Prix meeting 200m start alongside Michael Johnson, Linford Christie and Namibia's Frankie Frederiks, he figured he'd get 4th place.

The starting gun sounded and 20 seconds later, Johnson had won and Regis finished behind Frederiks and Christie in 4th place. When he thought about it afterwards, he realized that he had in fact created his own destiny through his thought process. In the week following, he trained not only his technique, but also his mind. He convinced himself that he can beat his rivals.

Ten days later, John Regis not only improved his race time by 0.8 of a second, he also won. This time it wasn't just a Grand Prix meeting. John Regis was now world 200m champion!

#72 YOU'RE NEVER BEATEN UNTIL YOU ADMIT IT

How can you maintain a winning attitude even when facing difficulties?

_____
_____
_____
_____
_____
_____
_____
_____
_____
_____
_____
_____
_____
_____
_____
_____

#73

THERE IS NO ELEVATOR TO SUCCESS. YOU HAVE TO TAKE THE STAIRS

Not only is taking the stairs good exercise (something that should be avoided the day before a big race though) but it is also akin to couple of aspects of peak performance.

Firstly, the stairs take time – so do results! Secondly, you need to focus on the nest step rather than look to the top of the flight. And thirdly, taking the stairs implies hard work. It implies making the difficult choice, avoiding the easy way out – doing what needs to be done.

By taking the stairs you say that you are taking control – no waiting around for others. You make it clear that your results are not at the mercy of things beyond your control.

You don't have to push buttons to get where you want to be – you just go there. When you want to!

#73 THERE IS NO ELEVATOR TO SUCCESS. YOU HAVE TO TAKE THE STAIRS

How can you embrace the journey and enjoy the process of climbing those stairs to success, as opposed to looking for the "elevator" or quick fix?

_____
_____
_____
_____
_____
_____
_____
_____
_____
_____
_____
_____
_____
_____
_____
_____
_____

#74

THERE ARE ONLY TWO OPTIONS REGARDING COMMITMENT. YOU'RE EITHER IN OR OUT. THERE'S NO SUCH THING AS A LIFE IN-BETWEEN

PAT RILEY

I know it is tough! As an amateur athlete you have to balance work, family and often friends with your training and sport "commitments". The only way to overcome this – apart from becoming a pro – is to manage your commitments.

In other words, you need to commit your mind and your body to one thing at a time. When you're at work, WORK. When you're at sport, leave everything else behind! This focus is the toughest part because I often find that my mind wanders between the two. I have some of my best business ideas while training – particularly swimming.

This happens because there's not much to concentrate on whilst doing endless laps of the pool so as my mind enters a state of relaxation, I become more creative and more adept at solving problems. For the most part though, you want to be a pig in every part of your life. Pigs are totally committed to the bacon on your plate. The chicken is only involved!

#74 THERE ARE ONLY TWO OPTIONS REGARDING COMMITMENT. YOU'RE EITHER IN OR OUT. THERE'S NO SUCH THING AS A LIFE IN-BETWEEN

Are you still fully committed to your current goals and endeavours?

_____
_____
_____
_____
_____
_____

What changes can you make to be more dedicated and focused on your path to success?

_____
_____
_____
_____
_____
_____
_____
_____
_____

#75

THERE ARE ONE HUNDRED AND NINETY NINE WAYS TO GET BEAT, BUT ONLY ONE WAY TO WIN; GET THERE FIRST

Tiger Woods said it… Second is the first loser! But for most of us the point is not to win, but to not get beaten. Take competitors out of the equation for a second.

Before you can beat others, you have to beat your inner demons. The inner voices, the excuses for not training, the lack of preparation, the lack of confidence, the equipment.

Only once you have achieved outstanding quality in your own performance can you begin to look besting others.

By only looking outward, at your competition, you give away the power within you. You give your competitors power over you – power they do not deserve. Excellence should be your first priority. Winning your next one.

#75 THERE ARE ONE HUNDRED AND NINETY NINE WAYS TO GET BEAT, BUT ONLY ONE WAY TO WIN; GET THERE FIRST

How can you be more proactive and seize opportunities before others do?

_____
_____
_____
_____
_____
_____
_____

In what areas of your life can you strive to be the first, not the last?

_____
_____
_____
_____
_____
_____
_____

#76

THERE ARE NO TRAFFIC JAMS ALONG THE EXTRA MILE

The road along the extra mile is a bit like Jo'burg roads during Christmas – clear and traffic free. The reason? Simple. There are very few people there. Most people seem to be content to go as far as the lack of pain and discomfort will take them.

If you choose to go further, expect results. If you choose to go beyond discomfort, beyond average dedication, you can also expect an uncluttered race – cause there aren't too many people at the front either!

#76 THERE ARE NO TRAFFIC JAMS ALONG THE EXTRA MILE

Where can you go the extra mile in your personal or professional life?

_____
_____
_____
_____
_____
_____
_____
_____

How can you stand out by exceeding expectations and putting in extra effort?

_____
_____
_____
_____
_____
_____
_____
_____

#77

GOLF IS A GAME WHOSE AIM IS TO HIT A VERY SMALL BALL INTO AN EVEN SMALLER HOLE, WITH WEAPONS SINGULARLY ILL-DESIGNED FOR THE PURPOSE

WINSTON CHURCHILL

Very often I find amateurs get too bogged down with equipment, what they ride, what they wear and how they look. In the mid-90's I remember a guy completing the Leppin Ironman in a jolly boat, a "dikwiel" and running the final leg in slops. In those days it was a canoe triathlon!

Why? To prove that it can be done.

The most important and powerful piece of equipment you own costs you nothing, will never break down and will never out live its usefulness. It sits between your ears.

It is your mind, because no action begins without a thought. These thoughts stimulate action-potential that move your muscles that get you to perform.

You don't need to top of the range equipment. It helps only because it allows you to feel better about yourself!

#77

GOLF IS A GAME WHOSE AIM IS TO HIT A VERY SMALL BALL INTO AN EVEN SMALLER HOLE, WITH WEAPONS SINGULARLY ILL-DESIGNED FOR THE PURPOSE

How do you handle challenging situations where you may not have the perfect tools or resources?

___

What creative approaches can you use to achieve your goals, even with limited resources?

#78

FOOTBALL DOESN'T BUILD CHARACTER. IT ELIMINATES WEAK ONES

DARRELL ROYAL

OK, not just football – any sport.

Before I do business with people, I try and get them out of the office onto the golf course, into the gym, onto their bikes (if they are remotely athletic). Because it is there where their true character reveals itself. People can't hide. This is where your true self emerges.

People of poor character don't last in sport – any sport, at any level! Success in the sports arena (however you define it) is the result of age-old values – honesty, hard-work, integrity, consequence and camaraderie. These are the people I want to surround myself with!

The same is, or should be, true in business.

#78 FOOTBALL DOESN'T BUILD CHARACTER. IT ELIMINATES WEAK ONES

Think about a challenging experience in your life. How did it shape your character?

_____
_____
_____
_____
_____
_____

How can you embrace adversity as an opportunity to strengthen your character and resilience?

_____
_____
_____
_____
_____
_____
_____
_____

#79

WHEN SOMEONE TELLS ME THERE IS ONLY ONE WAY TO DO THINGS, IT ALWAYS LIGHTS A FIRE UNDER MY BUTT. MY INSTANT REACTION IS, I'M GONNA PROVE YOU WRONG

PICABO STREET

Olympic Skiing gold medalists seldom appear to do things differently, but when a torn ACL and a femur crushing accident threaten to end your career – twice – Picabo was forced to look to a little extrinsic motivation.

This type of motivation can only come from people / structures you care about though. Coaches, mentors, wives, siblings and your kids can all help propel you to higher achievements. If you're famous, so can the media.

I spend a fair amount of time with "public" athletes helping them not to worry about the press though. That's seldom motivation and more often distraction. So are your fellow competitors and what they have to say. Keep the majority of your motivation internal and intrinsic. Only look beyond yourself if it is absolutely necessary!

#79

WHEN SOMEONE TELLS ME THERE IS ONLY ONE WAY TO DO THINGS, IT ALWAYS LIGHTS A FIRE UNDER MY BUTT. MY INSTANT REACTION IS, I'M GONNA PROVE YOU WRONG

Have you ever been told you can't do something a certain way? How did it motivate you?

_____
_____
_____
_____
_____
_____
_____

How can you use naysayers and challenges as fuel to prove them wrong and succeed on your terms?

_____
_____
_____
_____
_____
_____
_____
_____

#80

WHEN YOU GET INTO A TIGHT PLACE AND EVERYTHING GOES AGAINST YOU, TILL IT SEEMS AS THOUGH YOU COULD NOT HOLD ON A MINUTE LONGER, NEVER GIVE UP THEN, FOR THAT IS JUST THE PLACE AND TIME THAT THE TIDE WILL TURN

HARRIET BEECHER STOWE

Ah, heck! If everything in life was easy, life would be very boring. If events and trials were easy there'd be no honour and accomplishment in achieving them. It's only in pushing to the point of quitting, then not quitting and pushing through that we extend our boundaries, grow and leave a meaningful legacy. A life lived in complete comfort is wasted. A race completed in complete comfort is not a success.

Look at the faces of Olympic medallists just before the medal. Just before they cross the finish line. Just before the joy and elation of knowing they have gold. Those are not expressions of joy, relaxation and fun. Those are faces of pain, anguish and complete resilience. Only after that do we see the excitement, jubilation and celebration. They have these faces because they held on for that extra minute, second or split second. Their tide turned!

#80

WHEN YOU GET INTO A TIGHT PLACE AND EVERYTHING GOES AGAINST YOU, TILL IT SEEMS AS THOUGH YOU COULD NOT HOLD ON A MINUTE LONGER, NEVER GIVE UP THEN, FOR THAT IS JUST THE PLACE AND TIME THAT THE TIDE WILL TURN

Think about a challenging situation where you wanted to give up but didn't. How did the tide eventually turn in your favour?

How can you draw inspiration from your past resilience and use it to overcome current challenges?

#81

SUCCESS IS NOT TO BE PURSUED; IT IS TO BE ATTRACTED BY THE PERSON YOU BECOME
JIM ROHN

People often refer to sport stars as arrogant, ego-centric, selfish etc. However, I can't think that I've ever met a top athlete that is not friendly, easy to talk to and accessible – at the right time and place.

See, when you chase something selfishly, you may get it, but you will lose the person that you are.

When you stay true to who you are, attracting people and success through your actions and not pushing things away, you will get what you want, and you'll like yourself more!

#81 SUCCESS IS NOT TO BE PURSUED; IT IS TO BE ATTRACTED BY THE PERSON YOU BECOME

How can you focus on personal growth and self-improvement to naturally attract success?

_____
_____
_____
_____
_____
_____
_____

In what ways can you work on becoming the best version of yourself to invite success into your life?

_____
_____
_____
_____
_____
_____
_____

#82

SUCCESS ISN'T A RESULT OF SPONTANEOUS COMBUSTION. YOU MUST SET YOURSELF ON FIRE

Quite frankly I think that people who well themselves as "motivational speakers" should be taken to court and shown up for who they are – frauds. They may be excellent speakers, and they may get you off your butt for a day or two, maybe a week – but they can certainly never be regarded as a source of motivation!!

True motivation comes from within. From the fire you light in yourself on a daily basis. What the speakers do is influence what you are motivated to do! Not even the great sporting events you watch on TV can motivate you. Every year I watch Comrades, and every year I get motivated to run it the following year. But it's like a hot bath – the water gets cold in a few weeks and I return to multi-sport! VIVA.

#82 SUCCESS ISN'T A RESULT OF SPONTANEOUS COMBUSTION. YOU MUST SET YOURSELF ON FIRE

How can you actively work towards your aspirations and set yourself on fire with determination and enthusiasm?

#83

SUCCESS WITHOUT HONOUR IS AN UNSEASONED DISH; IT WILL SATISFY YOUR HUNGER, BUT IT WON'T TASTE GOOD
JOE PATERNO

One of the big problems in sport is that success is equated with podium finishes, winning and holding the trophy aloft.

When Baron Pierre de Coubertin founded the modern Olympic movement his vision was that of participation in the pursuit of improvement. Not winning at all costs.

When junior athletes are bought, sponsored obscenely and resort to banned substances the plot has been lost. When cyclists dope, teams refused entry to events, and illegal tactics are used to contrive success, then the honour has gone.

When there is no honour, there can be victory, but never success!

#83 SUCCESS WITHOUT HONOUR IS AN UNSEASONED DISH; IT WILL SATISFY YOUR HUNGER, BUT IT WON'T TASTE GOOD

Why is integrity and honour important in your pursuit of success?

_____
_____
_____
_____
_____
_____
_____

How can you ensure that your achievements are not only fulfilling but also aligned with your values and principles?

_____
_____
_____
_____
_____
_____
_____
_____

#84

WHEN IT'S ALL OVER, IT'S NOT WHO YOU WERE. IT'S WHETHER YOU MADE A DIFFERENCE
BOB DOLE

Athletes and top performers in any field are often seen as selfish and self-centred. In fact when Lance Armstrong got divorced, this was one of his "short-comings" that received some press coverage. The thing is that in order to consistently perform at a level above everyone else requires sacrifice. But when you don't like what you become in your quest for success, there is a problem.

Today true success and motivation does not come from being #1 anymore, or having more money, status and prestige. Research shows that it comes from feeling wanted, appreciated, loved and health.

Motivation today is about making a difference to someone else's life. It's about positively influencing the lives of the people around you!!

#84 WHEN IT'S ALL OVER, IT'S NOT WHO YOU WERE. IT'S WHETHER YOU MADE A DIFFERENCE

Reflect on the impact you've had on others and your community. How can you make a more significant difference?

_____
_____
_____
_____
_____
_____
_____

How can you leave a lasting legacy that goes beyond your individual accomplishments?

_____
_____
_____
_____
_____
_____
_____

#85

TAKE REST. A FIELD THAT HAS RESTED GIVES A BEAUTIFUL CROP

OVID

All too often we believe that the harder we train and the harder we work the better results we will get. Well that is only true up to a point. Everything needs balance in order to survive. Too much of anything is bad. The key is to know when to relax. When to rest. When to say NO.

Top performers know where to draw the line. When to put things off and when to put up their feet and rest. The world, your company, your sporting life will not come to an end when you rest and recharge for a while. Make sure you take regular breaks from whatever you are passionate about.

#85 TAKE REST. A FIELD THAT HAS RESTED GIVES A BEAUTIFUL CROP

When was the last time you allowed yourself to rest and recharge?

How can you incorporate regular periods of rest and self-care to improve your overall productivity and well-being?

#86

YOU LEARN YOU CAN DO YOUR BEST WHEN IT'S HARD, EVEN WHEN YOU'RE TIRED AND MAYBE HURTING A LITTLE BIT. IT FEELS GOOD TO SHOW SOME COURAGE

JOE NAMATH

The only thing that stops us going beyond the usual and the ordinary is fear.

Fear of success, fear of failure, fear of pain. It takes courage to push yourself beyond the pain threshold, but you will be surprised how much further your body can go when you take the inner voice of your mind out of the equation.

Now do one more lap, one more kilometre, one more rep. Breathe. Hold it. Last one…1…2…3. That's it.

#86 YOU LEARN YOU CAN DO YOUR BEST WHEN IT'S HARD, EVEN WHEN YOU'RE TIRED AND MAYBE HURTING A LITTLE BIT. IT FEELS GOOD TO SHOW SOME COURAGE

How can you find the strength and courage to do your best, even when faced with challenges and discomfort? Or when results aren't going your way?

#87

YOU MAY NOT REALIZE IT WHEN IT HAPPENS, BUT A KICK IN THE TEETH MAY BE THE BEST THING IN THE WORLD FOR YOU

WALT DISNEY

At school we're molly-coddled. Children and young athletes today have been brought up in an environment where there are no winners and losers and where not making the grade is met with acceptance and even sympathy.

The truth and nothing but the harsh truth is what we need to get back into high gear, to get focused, to get things done. All too often our performance is hampered by euphemisms. It's time to get real!!

We have a tendency to slack off in all areas of life and sometimes we need the brutal honesty of an honest, close and trusted friend or confidant.

#87 YOU MAY NOT REALISE IT WHEN IT HAPPENS, BUT A KICK IN THE TEETH MAY BE THE BEST THING IN THE WORLD FOR YOU

Think about a setback or failure that turned out to be a valuable lesson. How did it help you grow?

#88

YOU NEED TO PLAY WITH SUPREME CONFIDENCE, OR ELSE YOU'LL LOSE AGAIN, AND THEN LOSING BECOMES A HABIT

JOE PATERNO

It's actually contradictory. Self-confidence comes from repeatedly getting the results you want. The ones you work towards. But when you hit a road-block, or several failures one after the other, it's easy to begin to doubt yourself, your abilities and your persuasion.

When you experience a set-back, the best thing to do is to remind yourself of the successes you've had in the past. Learn from your failure, but don't dwell on it. Move on.

Reminding yourself of everything you have accomplished, allows your confidence to resurface. If you do this using visualisation techniques, you're actually stronger than before.

#88 YOU NEED TO PLAY WITH SUPREME CONFIDENCE, OR ELSE YOU'LL LOSE AGAIN, AND THEN LOSING BECOMES A HABIT

How can you build and maintain supreme confidence in your abilities and actions?

_____
_____
_____
_____
_____
_____
_____

In what areas of your life can you ensure that winning, not losing, becomes a habit?

_____
_____
_____
_____
_____
_____
_____

#89

THERE ARE SOME DEFEATS MORE TRIUMPHANT THAN VICTORIES

MICHEL DE MONTAIGNE

Not one super-successful person I know of has not experienced failure in the past. And we're not talking small ones either. The world marvels at the success of Elon Musk (and others) but we tend to forget, or not even know about, the failures and setbacks he had to overcome to get where they are today.

True learning and growth comes from figuring out what NOT to do, rather than only knowing what to do.

Truth be told, there are many ways to get the same positive results — some are easier than others, some are more fun than others. Negative results are always the product of the same mistakes.

#89 THERE ARE SOME DEFEATS MORE TRIUMPHANT THAN VICTORIES

Reflect on a time when a defeat led to personal growth and learning. How did it make you a better person?

_____
_____
_____
_____
_____
_____
_____

How can you embrace defeats as opportunities for triumph and self-improvement?

_____
_____
_____
_____
_____
_____
_____

#90

TAKE CARE OF YOUR BODY WITH STEADFAST FIDELITY. THE SOUL MUST SEE THROUGH THESE EYES ALONE, AND IF THEY ARE DIM, THE WHOLE WORLD IS CLOUDED
GOETHE

Ever noticed how your attention is drawn almost automatically to things you associate with – even subconsciously? When you first thought of buying that new bike, and you did because you liked it and not everyone rode one.

My wife bought a new car and one of the reasons she bought it was that she thought it was somewhat exclusive - a convertible that not everyone drives. A few days after she got it she complained to me that she now sees so many of them on the road!

Well it's not because there were suddenly more of that model on the road, she was just more focused on it. Whatever sport you're fanatical about will always seem to attract your attention in the media, on TV, and you definitely see more of your peers training than you do others. You get whatever your eyes and your soul focus on.

If your focus is unclear and hazy, so are your results.

#90 TAKE CARE OF YOUR BODY WITH STEADFAST FIDELITY. THE SOUL MUST SEE THROUGH THESE EYES ALONE, AND IF THEY ARE DIM, THE WHOLE WORLD IS CLOUDED

How can you prioritize self-care and physical well-being to maintain mental clarity and vision?

_____

What practices can you adopt to ensure your body and mind are in optimal condition for your personal and professional journey?

5

CHAPTER 5
FINAL THOUGHTS

FINAL THOUGHTS

There are admirable potentialities in every human being. Believe in your strength and your truth. Learn to repeat endlessly to yourself. "It all depends on me"

We know to do this, to try something new to take out performance to the next level. To create new physical and mental habits.

Too many of us leave our results up to others. When they don't deliver the best tactic and the easiest excuse is to blame them. "My coach didn't..." As we fail to take responsibility for what we do and blame others, we eventually lose faith in ourselves. We begin to believe that others do not have our best interests at heart. But why should they? They have, and rightly so, their interest at heart. You just happen to be part of their plan at the time. This is not a bad thing tough!!! Learn all you can.

The problem is that results, when we put our faith in what others will do for us, is that we lose faith in our own strength and abilities.

We begin to believe that our success rests in the hands of others. You need to take that power back! Right now. All your success rests squarely on your shoulders.

I hope that the 90 Mind Vitamins contained in this book have helped you build the daily foundation for peak performance. I know the daily journal opportunities have stimulated your thinking and helped you to look critically into how you can apply the insights created by these mind vitamins. Because just reading this book is not enough.

If you only read about the Mind Vitamins in this book but do nothing to action the insights, then is not a self-help book. It's a "shelf-help" book - it will only help to keep up your (book)shelf.

Dennis Waitley said that, *"The winners in life think constantly in terms of I can, I will, and I am. Losers, on the other hand, concentrate their waking thoughts on what they should have or would have done, or what they can't do."*

This book and journal combination will guide you to do just that. Life is too short for one sport. It's also too short for regrets. Young people I work with are always telling me about their dreams. The events they're going to enter, the equipment they want to buy, the challenges they want to complete. Older people also often talk to me and they're telling about the same things. They're not dreaming anymore though. They're saying "if only" they'd entered, if only they took the challenge, bought the gadget, took the trip!

Not that they're losers – they're just procrastinators. Live in the now. Start doing by changing the words you use. Improve your vocabulary, and start using an active rather than a passive voice. You will read this, you can do well , You are a success. You did after all win your very first race! You beat a couple of million other sperm!

Now it is up to you.

You would have completed your 90-day journey to your challenge or event. CONGRATULATIONS!!!

Please let me know how your event went and what successes you have achieved.

Erik Vermeulen

ONE LAST THING

As a conference Keynote speaker I have been sharing my experiences in leadership, from both a corporate and an adventure perspective with audiences on the global stage since 1999. I would love to share those and these Mind Vitamins with your organisation live and in-person.

Please reach out and let's chat about your requirements.

If you'd like to engage me, for a speaking engagement, a consulting partnership, or even just to share your experience, use the following contact points:

Telephone: +27 83 603-7119
E-mail: erik@ridgelineza.com
Website: www.ridgelineza.com
Facebook: Erik Vermeulen
LinkedIn: Erik Vermeulen

www.ingramcontent.com/pod-product-compliance
Lightning Source LLC
Chambersburg PA
CBHW080903230426
43663CB00014B/2608